W

Churchill, the
author, Church-
ill the brick-
layer, Churchill
the reader and
cigar-smoker in
those very rare
moments of
leisure afforded
to the present
occupant of 10,
Downing-
street.

... Churchill the
... author, Church-
...ure ... ill the brick-
...arily ... layer, Churchill
... not ... the reader and
... in all ... cigar-smoker in
...er Mr. ... those very rare
...d to re- ... moments of
...nompson ... leisure afforded
...ess. ... to the present

...d umbrella,
... something
... lethal. An
... is at once a
... and a piece
... only time he

There is a
tacit under-
standing be-
tween the
Prime Minister
and his shadow.
Winston
Churchill
has long ago
proved himself
as a man with-
out personal
fear. He will
visit places and
do things with-
out regard to
danger. But ...
he knows very
well that Walter
Thompson has
a job and a
responsibility to discharge. He
has never once made it difficult
for Thompson to carry out his
job.

...RCLAY

...ARR

... anybody with what
... was when, as the result of
... while cleaning it he
...self in the leg and was
... y for some months.

... was also in the days at the
... the last war that Inspector
...mpson had an experience with
... Churchill with which, as the
...ime Minister himself once said,
... we could both have well dis-
...ensed."

When a member of Lloyd
George's Cabinet, Mr. Churchill
was spending a few day: with
the Duke of Westminster at his
seat in the wilds of Sutherland-
shire. Lloyd George decided to
hold an emergency Cabinet meeting at Inverness. So from the
little town of Lairg, in a hired,
ramshackle car Mr. Churchill set
off, accompanied by Mr. Thompson, to reach Inverness by eight
o'clock that evening.

On a bleak road in the north
Inverness-shire winding round
the car went over the edge
...ed down till it came

Inspector Thompson, on the
other hand, as Mr. Churchill himself readily admits, has never
been fussy, never intruded himself, never been over-zealous.

The latest picture of Det.-Inspector Thompson,
following Mr. Churchill as the Prime Minister
went to Buckingham Palace to tender his
resignation.

...velled during this war without
Thompson. That was when the
Prime Minister went to Germany
this year and crossed the Rhine.
For there was an inviolable ru...
in force then—no civilians ...
lowed across the German fr...
tier.

And Detective Inspector ...
ter H. Thompson, in spite ...
lifelong work at Special ...
—tracking down and ...
German spies in the ...
campaigns against Anar...
all the varied work th...
ment undertakes—w...
just a civilian, un...
and Mussolini's, ...
shadows and body...
Gestapo, S.S., and ...
their fancy unifo...
holsters promine...

Once He Stayed

IN the air, on board
ship, in trains, on
the road, Walter
Thompson's eyes have
been wide open throughout the
hundreds of thousands of miles
that he and his charge have
travelled together, to Cairo,
Morocco, Teheran, Yalta, United

BESIDE THE BULLDOG

THE INTIMATE MEMOIRS OF
CHURCHILL'S BODYGUARD

V.E. Day: Churchill with Walter Thompson standing by his side.

BESIDE
THE
BULLDOG

THE INTIMATE MEMOIRS OF
CHURCHILL'S BODYGUARD

To Winston
with best wishes
Tommy

EX-DETECTIVE INSPECTOR
WALTER THOMPSON

INTRODUCTION BY LINDA STOKER,
THOMPSON'S GREAT-NIECE

APOLLO PUBLISHING

Published by Apollo Publishing Ltd, 17 Langbourne Mansions,
Langbourne Avenue, Highgate, London N6 6PR.

This publication reproduces in its entirety *Sixty Minutes with
Winston Churchill* by Walter Thompson, published by
Christopher Johnson Ltd, London, in 1953.

A copy of the British Library Cataloguing in Publication Data for this
title is available from the British Library.

Every effort has been made to contact copyright holders of material
reproduced in this book. If any have been inadvertently overlooked,
restitution will be made at the earliest opportunity.

First printing 2003

Printed in Spain

ISBN 0-9545223-0-3

Book designer: David Fordham
Copy-editor: Libby Willis
Aviation illustrator: Bernard Dow

CONTENTS

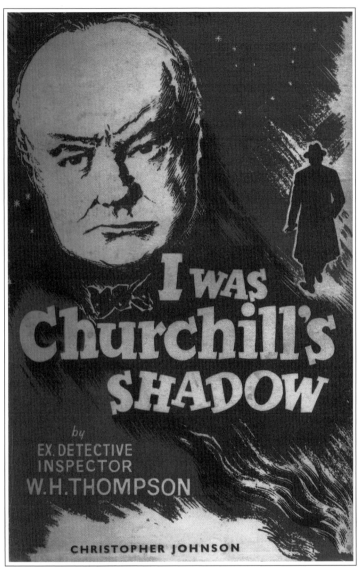

by
EX. DETECTIVE
INSPECTOR
W.H. THOMPSON

I WAS Churchill's SHADOW

CHRISTOPHER JOHNSON

First published in 1951, *I Was Churchill's Shadow*
is an intimate biography of Churchill during the war years.

INTRODUCTION

It was one of those dreary, unpromising afternoons when I stepped into the secondhand bookshop in Castle Cary, Somerset. The assistant smiled and I gave her one of those 'just looking' glances. I fumbled through the books, which appeared to be in no particular order, and my hand slid over one on the top of a pile. It was *Guard from the Yard* by Ex-Inspector Walter Thompson – my father's uncle and my great-uncle. I made the purchase, much to the delight of the shop assistant, who probably suspected me of loitering with intent to avoid boredom.

I already possessed one of my great-uncle's books, *I Was Churchill's Shadow*, but this one was new to me. It was fascinating, providing an intimate glimpse into his world of spies and special assignments. I was hooked. I needed to know more about my tall, handsome uncle, who in my childhood used to give me a pound note whenever I saw him – a very generous amount of money to give a child in those days.

Like many families, mine had disintegrated over the years. Uncle Walter (as we called him, though he was Tommy to his friends) had died sometime in the 1970s – I couldn't recall exactly when. He had had five children, so surely my second cousins must still be alive somewhere.

Unlike Churchill, Walter Thompson was always
impeccably turned out.

I could count Freddie out, as he had died heroically during the Second World War. But that left Harold, Harvey, Grace and Kathleen. The last I remembered of them was in the 1960s at Greatstone in Kent, when I had last seen Uncle Walter on a visit to my grandmother, his sister.

Since that unexpectedly seminal afternoon in Castle Cary, I have spent six years researching my uncle's life with Churchill. In 1999 I took up the job full time. Hidden away in dusty attics I have found old leather suitcases full of pictures and notes, original manuscripts, out-of-print books, letters, poems and scripts for radio. What struck me early on in my research was that my uncle's original notes and manuscripts omitted many of the stories we had been told as children about his exploits with Churchill.

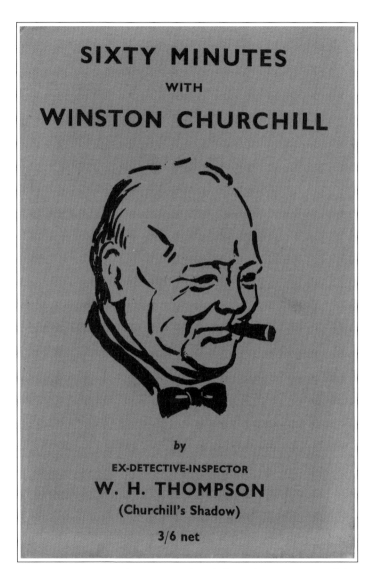

SIXTY MINUTES

WITH

WINSTON CHURCHILL

by

EX-DETECTIVE-INSPECTOR

W. H. THOMPSON

(Churchill's Shadow)

3/6 net

In *Sixty Minutes with Winston Churchill*, Walter recounts with pithy brevity the most remarkable stories from throughout his years with the great man.

One little book, though, did stand out as immensely interesting and unusually revealing. Published in 1953 as *Sixty Minutes with Winston Churchill*, it captured the intimacy of the relationship between these two very different men and dropped readers right into life at Churchill's elbow. How did my uncle come to enjoy such a close and rare connection with the man recently voted this country's greatest Briton?

In this Introduction I shall sketch in the background to Walter Thompson's extraordinary yet little-known role at the very centre of power during some of the most momentous times of the twentieth century. The constant stream of biographies and programmes about Churchill testifies to our enduring fascination with him. It seemed to me a great shame that this little gem of a book should have been long out of print and thus largely unavailable to Churchill's many admirers, so it is with enormous pleasure and excitement that I can now lay its delights before them in this new edition.

```
AUGUST 22nd 1939
TELEGRAM
MEET ME CROYDON AERO-
DROME 4.30PM WEDNESDAY
CHURCHILL
```

"Strange order for a grocer," Walter (Tommy) Thompson was to write later. It was 1939 and he had retired from Special Branch three years earlier.

He had lived a hectic life at the side of Lloyd George and Winston Churchill as a police bodyguard for twenty-three years in all, twelve of them with Churchill. Now his livelihood was the little grocery store that had been his wife Kate's dream. For Tommy it was fulfilling a duty after years of absence. Pages in the diary he kept of his life appeared blank during these years, apart from the date and the odd list of groceries.

How could anything compare to protecting Churchill from assassins and mobs and sharing the unorthodox routine of the man? Now he was excited at the possibility of meeting Churchill again. What he did not know was that within days he would be protecting one of the world's greatest men during one of the world's worst conflicts.

Tommy's words bring their meeting vividly before our eyes:

I was at Croydon aerodrome the next afternoon, full of excitement and curiosity. The Paris plane came in, and out bounded Mr. Churchill. He was looking fit and full of energy as usual, but his expression was grim. He smiled when he saw me. I waited for some explanation of the summons. But all he said was, "Hallo Thompson. Nice to see you. Get the baggage together and bring it on to Chartwell."

Tommy might well have been hurt by Churchill's remarks. He would have wanted to know why Churchill had thought it so important to call him at short notice; instead he had been treated as a servant. Perhaps the sight of Churchill's latest secretary, Mary Shearburn, descending the steps of the plane prevented Tommy from protesting. She was a handsome young woman with a flashing smile and was to figure significantly in Tommy's life later.

Churchill's explanation that afternoon at Chartwell was typically clear and to the point. "The Germans believe I am one of their most formidable enemies. They will not stop short of assassination. I can look after myself in the daytime. Will you protect me at night?"

Churchill had been in France working on support for his personal campaign against Hitler. Mary Shearburn noted his words as they travelled in the car. Admiring the fields of wheat and barley Churchill had remarked, "Before the harvest is gathered in, we shall be at war." She added that he became very sombre: "There would be no further dictation that day."

Churchill was on his way to visit the Duke of Windsor in the south of France when he was warned that his life

14

Within weeks of V.E. Day, Walter made
Churchill's former secretary, Mary Shearburn,
his second wife.

was in danger. He flew back to England, sending the
telegram to Tommy on the way. It did not take Tommy
long to make up his mind. As he wrote in *I Was Churchill's
Shadow*, "What greater honour could be bestowed upon
me than to be asked to make myself responsible for the
personal safety of this great man, at a time when so much
depended upon his maintaining his strength and
vigour?"

Churchill offered Tommy £5 per week to act as his
private personal bodyguard. He handed him his Colt
automatic and then promptly forgot about any threats
and the safety of his life. Those worries were now

delegated to the one man Churchill utterly relied upon, the one man he knew would stand in front of a bullet for him: Walter Thompson.

As Tommy returned home on the train that evening he must have wrestled with his conscience over how he was to explain to Kate that his old boss (now out of office) wanted him back on guard duty. We can only surmise what Kate's feelings must have been on hearing the news, but Tommy evidently prevailed, and each evening after the grocery closed, Tommy headed for Chartwell.

After patrolling the grounds with a gun, Tommy would conduct an all-night vigil inside the house while Churchill worked and slept. In the notes that were to become the manuscript of *I Was Churchill's Shadow*, Tommy evoked those eerie days before the storm: "I lived this strange role of an armed unofficial bodyguard patrolling around the quiet of the Kentish countryside in peacetime ready to pounce on a would-be Nazi murderer."

This bizarre part-time job was not to last, for on the Saturday of that same week in August 1939 a state of emergency was declared by the government. Reservists from all services were instructed to rejoin their units and Tommy reported to Scotland Yard for police duties in accordance with the agreement he had made with his commander when he retired.

Churchill was not prepared to exchange for a younger version the man he trusted with his life. He telephoned Sir Philip Game, Commissioner of Police, and had Tommy assigned to him officially. His appointment was meant to be secret, and a request was made to the newspapers that Thompson never be referred to nor any photographs of Churchill with Tommy be published. Yet Tommy told us that within days a well-known newspaper announced his appointment.

I made a guess that the leak would have come from one of Churchill's closest friends, Lord Beaverbrook, who owned the *Daily Express*. Sure enough, I was delighted to discover an article with a picture of Tommy in silhouette in the *Express* in the Newspaper Library in Colindale, London. Printed on 12th February and entitled "Churchill finds his Shadow Again," it read:

> Mr Winston Churchill has got back his "Shadow" – Inspector W. H. Thompson of the Special Branch of Scotland Yard. Thompson had retired from the police force, but he rejoined for the war and was asked for again by the First Lord of the Admiralty to act as his personal detective.
>
> In future wherever Mr Churchill goes – by air, ship or car – he will be accompanied by this tall, clean-shaven man.

The appointment must have been a relief for Tommy, for now he had no choice but to take up the job he loved, the job that had been his life. "It was a return to duty for a friend," he wrote. But there was much more than just friendship in the relationship between Tommy and Churchill.

He captured its essence when he wrote in *Guard from the Yard*: "When I first became Mr Churchill's personal detective in 1921, I had found his manner, brusque, off-handed – even, as I thought then, piggish. But I soon began to see through the rough façade, to wait for the grimness to break up in that boyish smile. It did not take

me long to like him. In a little while I came to love him." In fact, their relationship was so close that Tommy called Churchill "Father" in private.

The very nature of Tommy's job made him the one person who was always in Churchill's presence. Once Churchill realised that Tommy was an intelligent and thoughtful fellow, he used him to bounce ideas off before taking them to Parliament or the nation. To the outside world Tommy appeared a silent, faceless bodyguard but in reality he was a sounding-board, a confidant and a pal. Only Churchill's closest friends were aware of Tommy's importance. When writing about these friends, Tommy noted that they all treated him with the "greatest kindness and consideration". Indeed, they respected Tommy's pragmatism and that he was not afraid to challenge Churchill. In his notes Tommy observed, "I have been greatly privileged in being allowed to express myself to him very strongly in the matter of various escapades on which he has embarked." In *I Was Churchill's Shadow* he reveals a perceptive understanding of Churchill's character: "He likes to get his own way, but he is far more tolerant of those who stand up to him than he is of the sycophant."

Picture the scene: an old man (Churchill was sixty-five) aspiring to the top job in the country with a bodyguard who was past his prime at forty-nine years old. But it was the old man who wore out his bodyguard each day. Tommy admitted in *I Was Churchill's Shadow* that "his impulsiveness and tireless energy made me have to fight to keep up with him."

Churchill's protection was always a difficult job for Tommy. First there were many plots to assassinate him.

In 1943, as Churchill emerges from the House of Commons,
Ottawa, Walter hangs back and scans the area
for dangers.

Then there was the odd "nut" who felt he or she would have a go. Compounding these was Churchill's unorthodox style. He liked to meet the people – he was a very public figure and enjoyed the energy of crowds. Where President Roosevelt had thirty or more bodyguards with him everywhere he went, Churchill had just Tommy and sometimes Cyril Davies, Tommy's sergeant.

As children we always enjoyed watching *All Our Yesterdays* on the television because we played a family game called Spot Uncle Walter. I usually won because I was best at detecting the tall man who was not looking at the camera or at Churchill, but at the windows of surrounding buildings and at the crowd.

Tommy returned Churchill's Colt to him on 27th August 1939 and requisitioned a Webley .32. He had a special patent leather holster so the gun would be just inside his jacket between the second and third buttons; he told us later that he could draw faster from this position than from a shoulder holster. But when Churchill walked among crowds, Tommy would hold the gun in his overcoat pocket. He was ever vigilant.

Back in the saddle Tommy's first challenge was a psychological one. He had to convince Churchill that if he was to delegate his personal safety to him, he needed to listen to him and obey his instructions – Churchill had been difficult on his first assignment but now the threat was heightened. On 3rd September 1939 war was declared. Minutes after Chamberlain's eleven o'clock radio broadcast to the nation, the first air-raid warning sounded. Tommy described Churchill's response in *I Was Churchill's Shadow*: "He stalked to the entrance to the flats [Churchill's home in Morpeth Mansions, London] and stared up into the sky like a warhorse scenting battle." Tommy wanted Churchill to go to the air-raid shelter and was quick-witted enough to persuade him that he ought to set an example to his family and his staff. Churchill hated being manipulated, and he snatched a bottle of brandy before leading the party to the basement that had been prepared. Tommy recalled him in the shelter "prowling around like a caged animal".

Churchill loathed air-raid shelters and played games with Tommy on many occasions to avoid being caged. He loved to stand on the roof of his apartment and "watch the fireworks", as he called them. Tommy's solution was to have an air-raid shelter built of sandbags on the roof. When Churchill refused to use it, Tommy recruited Clementine Churchill to help. She made Winston give his promise that he would go down to the shelter to sleep. One night Churchill put on his pyjamas, went down to the shelter and climbed into bed. Ten minutes later he reappeared and announced to the outfoxed Tommy: "I have kept my word. I came downstairs to go to bed. Now I am going upstairs to work."

Tommy had ultimate authority for Churchill's travel arrangements and he masterminded clever ways of getting Churchill wherever he needed to be and confusing the enemy. This was aided by the Secret Service recruiting a

number of doubles for Churchill and later for Tommy, too. One of the most important of these was Churchill's radio double, Norman Shelley. I always thought that Shelley, an actor, should have asked for royalties on the "We will fight them on the beaches" speech. Television and radio stations have broadcast that speech, read by Shelley, over and over again. Churchill had made the speech earlier in the House of Commons but it is Norman we hear telling the nation:

> We shall defend our island, whatever the cost may be, we shall fight on the beaches, we shall fight on the landing grounds, we shall fight in the fields and in the streets, we shall fight in the hills: we shall never surrender.

It still gives me shivers to read it, more than sixty years later. Churchill had rehearsed his words and his timing well, with both Tommy and his secretary Mary Shearburn appraising his performance late into the evening. Churchill listened to Shelley's repetition of it on the radio and commented to Tommy that it was "jolly good", and that he might as well do all his broadcasts in the future. This enabled Churchill to be in places other than the BBC Studios in Portland Place on many occasions.

The first opportunity for deception arose when Churchill went to France in the first week after the outbreak of war. His mission was to encourage the French to stay in the war. The perception that Churchill was still in London proved very helpful during all the trips he was to make.

On one occasion Tommy decided it was too dangerous for Churchill to travel, and personally made sure that he could not. It was in North Africa in June 1943. After the conference with Generals Giraud and de Gaulle in Algiers, General Ike Eisenhower wanted Churchill off his hands. He pushed for Churchill to leave so that he would not have responsibility for his life. Tommy knew that the Germans were planning an assassination attempt and that they were well aware by now of his trick of switching to commercial aircraft. He did not want Churchill to be flying the next day, so he drove for two hours to the airport and removed a part from the plane.

The most serious German assassination attempt was made at the Great Powers Conference in Teheran in 1943. Stalin invited Roosevelt to join him at the Russian Embassy, which was next door to the British legation where Churchill was installed. The German plan was bungled, though, and no harm came to any of the Allied leaders.

Tommy's sixth sense was working well. He was uneasy about the journey back to the airport in the convoy of cars and at the last moment pulled Churchill from his official vehicle. He let the cars go then found a battered old Army vehicle at the rear of the legation. Having strapped some old suitcases to the roof, he set off with Churchill and a Russian-speaking driver on the back road to the airport. Churchill lit a cigar in the back, but Tommy understandably protested. "Sir, the cigar, it's a dead giveaway!"

Churchill grunted and tossed the cigar out of the window – he objected to any disruption to his pleasures. Tommy was pleased with his deception, commenting later, "We drove quietly through Teheran on our own. Nobody gave us a second glance."

Churchill's life was constantly in danger. One Secret Service agent wrote to Churchill on 28th February 1951, "I have it on the authority of General Erwin Lahousen, Deputy Chief of German Intelligence, that Hitler gave orders for an attempt to be made on your life."

Tommy was much more than just a quick-witted detective. He was a man with a big heart, and his love for Churchill went far beyond the normal call of duty. He protected him from people when he was depressed. He understood Churchill's black moods and was a lively, happy soul himself so was never affected by them. He knew how to work on Churchill gently to lift him out of his depression. He tolerated Churchill's outbursts, he listened to Churchill's tantrums – the sort that a child feels safe enough to have only with its mother. He let him blow off steam until he was exhausted and then would carry him to bed and sit in the chair beside him all night long, protecting his life but also ensuring his sleep was not disturbed.

He made certain that no one observed Churchill's manic behaviours. Tommy wrote these off as a necessary part of the character of Churchill the leader. He told us that he thought they gave Churchill relief from his overtaxed mind. One interesting habit was his manic marching, often to popular music. Tommy would patiently wait outside the room, preventing anyone, of whatever rank, from entering.

Churchill had no qualms about encumbering Walter with his personal belongings.

Tommy monitored Churchill's health constantly and reported any changes to Lord Moran, his physician. It was not difficult to see that Churchill was exhausted after the Teheran Conference in November 1943. He arrived at Tunis looking drawn and Tommy alerted Moran, but the doctor insisted Churchill was just tired. Tommy made sure that Churchill went straight to bed and regularly took his temperature, which was rising fast. He suspected Churchill had pneumonia and stayed with him all night listening to the tempo of his breathing. About two o'clock in the morning Churchill's breathing seemed to have stopped. "I do not remember in my life such a feeling of shock and fear," Tommy later recorded. Yet the stillness signified recovery rather than the reverse, for when Tommy listened again, with his head close to Churchill's pillow, he heard steady and quiet breathing in place of the "fast, stertorous" sounds that had rent the air before. In the morning Churchill said to Tommy, "I am tired out in body, soul and spirit. All is planned and ready. In what better place could I die than here – in the ruins of Carthage?"

This incident illustrates what an immense responsibility Tommy bore, which he shouldered with pride, devotion and a remarkably unflappable commonsense approach. What made Tommy such a dedicated, loyal bodyguard and such a pillar of strength for Churchill? I certainly recognise some of his sterling qualities as family traits. For instance, even as children we were always taught to be assertive, while the care and kindness that Tommy lavished on Churchill are familiar to me from my grandmother, his sister.

But how did this uneducated man from a humble background come to be guarding Churchill during the war? A resumé of Tommy's background helps explain how he came to be a central figure in Churchill's life.

Walter Henry Thompson was born in 1890 in Brixton, south London, one of thirteen children of working-class parents. His Presbyterian father was an insurance agent, his Jewish mother was from a rather more wealthy family than his father's but at the time of Tommy's birth she was

running a sweet shop in the nearby park. Always energetic, Tommy played with the local children in the park and showed promise as a footballer, though the family was so poor that he had to drill holes in an ordinary pair of boots and fit his own studs – an early indication of the resourcefulness and refusal to be beaten by circumstances that Churchill was to value so highly. At eighteen he played semi-professional football for a London team.

His prowess on the pitch was not quite matched in the classroom, and his simple education ended when he was eleven. He began full-time employment as a clerk in Leadenhall Market at the age of twelve, probably working for a friend or relative of the family. He ran errands and kept simple ledgers, but it is likely that his duties did not suit him at all. Luckily, another career path was to open up quite by chance.

One lunchtime, while Tommy was wandering in the market, idly looking at the stalls, a mêlée of men spewed out of a pub. Looking up, he realised they were attacking a policeman. He launched himself into the fracas and rescued the battered officer. A few days later he received a letter of thanks and a medal from the police force, and he immediately decided he would like a career in which he could use his fists. He joined up and became PC 549 of Paddington Green Police Station.

Recalling his early training Tommy wrote later, "We learn by boxing and ju-jitsu to handle those who disturb the King's peace. And we learn the various tricks of our trade by which policemen acquire that sixth sense." He became a beat bobby and enjoyed his work. In 1911 he married Kate, his long-standing girlfriend, in a simple ceremony in a Presbyterian church in Leytonstone, East London.

P.C. 549 of Paddington Green Station. Walter as a
"man in blue" before his 1913 promotion to Special Branch.

In 1913 a rare opportunity came his way. At the morning parade at Paddington Green one day, the Acting Sergeant announced that Scotland Yard was asking for volunteers for Special Branch. New recruits were needed, he explained, "so we can be one jump ahead of those seeking women's suffrage". He told the assembled men that an examination would be held the next day for those wishing to be considered as applicants. Certain educational qualifications would be required. Police officers interested should hand in their names on returning from their beats if they proposed to apply for a transfer.

As Tommy marched off the parade ground, he heard another policeman in the file whisper, "Thompson won't go for it – he hasn't got sufficient education." This laid down the gauntlet for Tommy, but he, too, was concerned about his poor education.

That evening on the beat in Covent Garden, Tommy noticed that the driver of a cart was asleep. He stepped into the road and brought the horse to a halt. The abrupt end to the rhythm that had lulled the driver off to sleep woke him up, and he exclaimed, "Cor 'strewth, guv'nor! Fancy you noticing that! You oughter been a detective, not a policeman."

Galvanised by this, Tommy decided to have a go after all at really becoming a detective. He discovered that Scotland Yard was looking for thirteen new Special Branch

men. "I knew this was a good omen," he wrote, "as I am one of thirteen children and it has always been my lucky number."

The tests were rigorous and required a high degree of literacy, observational skills and memory. He described in detail in *Guard from the Yard* the Picking your Man test he undertook at Peel House. "I was given a brief description of a man to study. Then I was shown into a room where about thirty ordinary-looking individuals were walking up and down. 'You've got thirty seconds to find your man,' I was told. I had received some training in the art of recognition before this test. For instance, to divide the face into quarters (left side, right side, top half, lower half) and to study these at all angles and memorise them. Later I learnt that a man may alter his nostrils, hide his mouth with a moustache, blow out his cheeks – even cut off his ears – but you can still pick him out by his brow."

He had to wait for several painful weeks before he heard the result. "I almost gave up in despair, thinking that I could not have passed." After all, many of the other candidates had enjoyed a secondary education. But he was successful, and in the spring of 1913 he wrote in the notes that were to form the basis of *Guard from the Yard*: "I am a detective constable in the Special Branch, New Scotland Yard; having survived several months of intensive training and scrutiny by my chiefs."

Guard from the Yard is also where he explained the difference between a criminal detective and a "Special":

The Special Man has to tread a deal more softly and understand the art of the soft tongue that turneth away wrath – and incidentally puts a suspect off his guard! Whereas the ordinary detective can always feel the law stands behind him, the Special more often than not has to work without this advantage. An indiscretion puts not only himself but his chief and possibly his government into "the soup". The situations he has to face are packed with variety and always present new problems. The young aspirant to this Branch has got to show his superiors that in the near future he will acquire tact, discretion, patience, firmness and an even temper in the most uncomfortable circumstances.

All of this early training was to be invaluable in the great task that was to lie ahead of him.

His first assignment was to keep tabs on the Suffragettes. One incident he wrote about in these early days is a charming vignette that reveals Tommy's instinctive chivalry and gives us a glimpse of his easy

rapport with the opposite sex. When he was following one of the Pankhurst daughters home, it began to rain. "She realised she was being followed," he wrote in *Guard from the Yard*, "and as it began to pour with rain, she looked round at me in an enquiring manner. She was wearing very summery attire. I walked up beside her and we shared my umbrella. Eventually I escorted her home, quite enjoying that excessively moist day."

As war with Germany approached in 1914, Tommy's unit began to take an interest in the activities of a large number of foreign agents in touch with the government of Kaiser William II. "The watching never relaxed until the day that war broke out," he recalled later.

A huge dossier of information, which covered all parts of the country, was compiled:

> Practically every "ordinary" agent had been cornered and assessed for his or her value, and this led us as intended to the "principals" – the only ones who really mattered. Thanks to this laborious work, within twelve hours following the declaration of war on 4th August 1914 the German espionage system in Great Britain had been smashed. It was the most elaborate history had ever seen. In those few hours just on five hundred hostile agents were arrested. That was a hectic night I never forgot.

Tommy's new assignment was to seek and arrest German agents; he even had a double agent living with him in his home. "He was never to leave my sight," Tommy remembered. "He was quite a pleasant-looking, fair-haired young man who spoke good English but was not talkative. He used to stay in my sitting room all day drawing diagrams. After a week or so he showed me detailed sketches of German aeroplanes, Zeppelins and other equipment." Tommy waited patiently while the German finished his work and then escorted him to a steamer ship that took him to the United States.

On being transferred to Southampton docks, Tommy was detailed to look out for enemy agents entering and leaving the country. In his memoirs he recalled one especially intriguing episode:

One Saturday evening a tall, handsome young Belgian lady, extremely elegant, presented her passport to me. She wanted to leave on the outgoing Channel boat. Certain signs did not satisfy me and her baggage was very scanty, which was always regarded as suspicious. After a search we had her brought in for special examination. She sat in front of six of us, perfectly at her ease, answering questions as fast as they could be put to her. Sometimes her eyes flashed or she smiled enigmatically. Somehow there was always something empty and elusive about her answers, which made us go on. We started at 7 p.m. and went on till 11 p.m., when her boat left; then we decided to detain her and reopen the examination on Sunday morning. We opened at 10 a.m. on Sunday and were still going strong at 1 p.m. By that time she was much the least disturbed of the lot. We had learnt absolutely nothing about her. She was the cleverest woman I have met. Then we learnt the truth. She was one of our own agents bound for Belgian occupied areas!

Thus Tommy was to have quite a grounding in spies and assassination plots before he took on his final job of guarding Churchill. He was part of the team that during the First World War rounded up spies such as Carl Lody, Rosenthal and Müller.

After the war Tommy was promoted in 1920 to Detective Sergeant. He had a new and prestigious assignment: Lloyd George. "So you are to be my newest guardian angel?" was how the Prime Minister greeted Tommy upon his appointment. "I hope I don't give you too much trouble. I believe I am apt to be a bit troublesome at times!" But Lloyd George was not at all troublesome – not like the other statesman who was to come into Tommy's care.

Tommy held Lloyd George in high esteem. In *Guard from the Yard* he reflected:

> The strange inner power of this man was always making itself felt to those around him. He was the very spirit of good humour. You might swear murder against the PM but when you had been talking with him for a few minutes you would change your mind to the other extreme. Off duty he was an entirely simple and charming man, almost ordinary in fact, except for his restlessness... As one who saw him so much in his home circle, it seemed to me that when he came to face affairs of state he rose on to an entirely different and high plane. His whole being – physical and mental – seemed to change in a way impossible to define. It seemed as if the fire had suddenly blazed up inside.

Tommy's private observations of the famous people he guarded give us a new and privileged insight into what

Lloyd George, to whom Walter was assigned in 1920.

Walter's three sons, Harold (top left), Freddie (top right),
and Harvey. One of the first Pathfinders,
Freddie went missing over enemy territory in
March 1943.

they were really like. As with Lloyd George, he shares with us Churchill's inner thoughts, his wicked sense of humour and his despair. His unique proximity and perspective, and his natural talent for relating charming little anecdotes absent from most other accounts, wonderfully enhance our appreciation of Churchill the man as well as Churchill the legend.

Tommy was assigned to Churchill in February 1921 and, off and on, was Churchill's official or unofficial bodyguard until June 1945. (He worked for Churchill unofficially just before war broke out, as we have seen, and also in 1930–32 when Churchill was out of office but by "a unique arrangement" Tommy was assigned to accompany him to the United States.) Tommy's memoirs record his initial reaction to the new appointment: "I was suddenly instructed to take up protection duty with Mr Winston Churchill. [Churchill was then Minister of Air.] I was filled with dismay, because there was a belief among us that he was an extremely difficult man to guard and rather uncertain in mood."

Tommy acted as Churchill's shadow continuously for the next eight and a half years, and despite his early qualms, it proved "the most interesting and pleasant (if strenuous) period of my career".

A few weeks into this new appointment, Tommy was told he would have to accompany Churchill on his official tour of what he described as the "Near East". "So far, I had not hit it off very well with Winston and I was a bit depressed," he admitted later. "The truth was that he was one of those dynamic persons with original ways, who need getting used to." At this time Tommy would have been thirty-one and his uncharacteristic low spirits might have been due to

reluctance to leave behind his pregnant wife and three young sons, Harold, six, Freddie, four, and Harvey, two. In the event, thrust into strange surroundings far from their home turf, the tour proved a welcome opportunity for the two men to get to know each other and establish the ground rules upon which their rock-solid relationship was to grow. As Churchill observed at one point, "We're just beginning to understand each other."

Tommy retired in 1936 with a pension of £207, 7d per annum. He bought a grocer's store in South London and settled into the life his wife Kate had always dreamed about. Gone were the days of protecting the man he loved day and night. At last he would have the chance to be a family man. But Tommy was certainly not as happy as his wife had hoped he would be. He found the routine of life, with regular sleeping hours and always waking up in the same bed, difficult. He was bored and thought his life was over. But then in 1939 that tantalising telegram arrived. The rest, as they say, truly is history…

LINDA STOKER
Walter Thompson's Great-Niece
MAY 2003

Churchill in his siren suit.

Mr. and Mrs. Churchill alight from a train
in Nova Scotia in 1943. Ever watchful, Walter scours the
station building for assassins.

What follows reproduces the
entire text of

SIXTY MINUTES
WITH
WINSTON
CHURCHILL

by WALTER THOMPSON

originally published by Christopher Johnson Ltd,
London, 1953

Footnotes (in brown type)
are by Linda Stoker

INTRODUCTION BY
WALTER THOMPSON

THE success of my book *I Was Churchill's Shadow* has led me to gather together this collection of anecdotes about Mr. Winston Churchill. I have excluded all of the many stories about Mr. Churchill with which I am familiar but which did not occur in circumstances for which I can vouch from my personal experience.

It has been my privilege to serve the greatest Englishman of this generation during three periods. I was detailed to guard him as a member of the Special Branch at Scotland Yard from 1921 until he ceased to hold office in the Baldwin Government in 1929, during his visit to the United States in 1931–32 and from August 1939 until after the end of the war in Europe.

In *I Was Churchill's Shadow* I dealt with only the last of these three periods. Now I am able to include many incidents that happened during my service with Mr. Churchill before 1939.

My own recollections in writing this book have been stimulated by those of my wife, formerly Miss Mary Shearburn, who acted as secretary to Mr. Churchill for some years.

I am indebted to Messrs. Jarrolds Publishers Ltd. for permission to use certain material, and to Mr. Ivor R. M. Davies for editorial assistance.

THE FIRST MEETING

I<small>T WAS</small> a temporary appointment that lasted for nine and a half years. I was recalled to service with Winston Churchill in 1939 and served with him another six years. I was reluctant to join him, for Mr. Churchill had the reputation of being a difficult charge. I only found him so occasionally! I regret not a minute of the time I spent with him and have reason, too, to believe that he was not dissatisfied for he has shown me great kindness and appreciation. What greater privilege could fall to the lot of a police officer than to have the responsibility for the safety of the greatest Englishman of his generation?

I became a Detective Sergeant of the Special Branch at Scotland Yard in February 1920, and within a few days was employed on protective duty with the Prime Minister, Mr. Lloyd George. In the spring of the following year I was transferred to the service of Mr. Winston Churchill, on the understanding that I was to remain with him for a few weeks only.

He lived at that time in Sussex Square, and when I first called upon him there to discuss our routine together it was revealed to me that, whatever others said, here was a man in whom I could have confidence and whom I might grow to love.

My first conversation with him took place in his study, a sparsely furnished room surrounded by well-filled bookcases. As he talked to me, his stocky figure paced up and down the room with his hands clasped behind his back. From time to time he lifted his head and shot a shrewd, penetrating glance at me. He asked me to tell

Churchill's determination and warmth
were immediately apparent.

him simply how I conceived the nature of my duties and, while I did so, he was obviously summing me up. He must have been satisfied, for he dismissed me by thrusting out his hand and saying, with a smile that lit up his face, "Thank you very much, Thompson. I have no doubt that we shall get on well together."

Before I left the room, he had resumed his restless pacing up and down the floor.

ALONE IN CAIRO

Soon after my appointment to Mr. Churchill's staff, in February 1921, we proceeded to Egypt, where, in his capacity as Secretary of State for Air, Churchill was to inspect units of the Royal Air Force. He was accompanied by Lord Trenchard, his Parliamentary Private Secretary, Sir Archibald Sinclair, and the legendary T. E. Lawrence of Arabia.

The Egyptian Nationalists took this opportunity to demonstrate their opposition to the British connection, and numerous ugly incidents took place as the cars proceeded through the main Egyptian towns.

In Cairo we stayed at the Semiramis Hotel and, as soon as we got there, I was called aside by the head of the Egyptian police, Russell Pasha. He talked to me in the gravest possible tones, saying, "Churchill is in the greatest danger. Trust nobody; black or white. Guard him to the exclusion of everything else."

With this warning ringing in my ears, I went straight up to Winston's room and found him sitting at a table writing.

"Is everything in order, sir?" I queried.

He smiled, "Stop worrying, Thompson. I am all right. Go and have a wash before dinner."

As I went to do so, I told the doorkeeper to report to me if anything the slightest bit untoward occurred.

Within five minutes, my door burst open and I was informed, "He's gone out – by himself – on foot."

Churchill was on his way to see General Allenby, heedless of the extreme danger he was in. I caught him

47

Accompanying Churchill and Sir Archibald Sinclair in Cairo.

up on the way. I had been frightened. Now I was angry. I said, all in a burst, "We can't have this, sir. I can't guard you if you treat me like this, sir. I've a great responsibility, and you are making my job quite impossible."

I waited apprehensively for the reply which, when it came, was the soft answer that turneth away wrath. "I will do all that I can to help you, Thompson. We're just beginning to understand each other."

Churchill never uses his position to browbeat you if he considers that you are justified in your attitude.

Tommy refers to "numerous ugly incidents". At one point he and an R.A.F. sergeant fought off a mob that had surrounded Churchill's car. Earlier, as they were leaving Alexandria on the Sultan's white train, hordes of angry men had stoned the train and smashed every window. Tommy tried to fight off men attempting to enter the carriage with the butt of his gun but he was overwhelmed. A small man in Arab robes appeared at the door of Churchill's carriage and raised his hand to the crowd. Immediately the riot stopped and the people gave an audible gasp. It was T. E. Lawrence, better known as Lawrence of Arabia. The train gathered enough steam to pull away safely and take Churchill onwards to Cairo.

A Camel Corps

With Mr. Churchill and T. E. Lawrence in 1921, I set off in an official party of about twenty to ride a camel from the Pyramids to Sakara. We were told that the journey would take about two and a half hours.

The camels were provided by the Egyptian Camel Corps and we were accompanied by a motley collection of Arab dignitaries on their splendid stallions. They made a colourful party.

Galloping on a camel is not my idea of pleasure. It resembles being turned round in a milk churn at fast speed. Nevertheless, gallop I had to – if I was going to keep up with Mr. Churchill. He entered into the spirit of the matter with boyish zest and everything proceeded satisfactorily if somewhat hectically, until the British statesman fell off his camel.

I was alarmed, for Mr. Churchill lay quite still on the ground, and was surrounded by the Arabs on their steeds shouting out all kinds of advice. It seemed to me that he was in imminent danger of being trampled to death by the horses. Winston was the least concerned person there. He soon got to his feet and, in spite of offers to give him a horse, insisted on remounting the camel.

T. E. Lawrence had difficulty in containing his laughter. He told Churchill, "It was only to be expected you know, Winston. The old camel blew himself out when he heard that he was to have the honour of carrying such a great man, but when he saw the way that you ride he decided that he must have been misinformed. He deflated himself and the saddle girth slipped round, throwing you."

When we reached Sakara, I had had enough of riding camels to last me the rest of my life. I looked forward to making the return journey by car.

Lawrence and Churchill had other ideas, though. They were quite willing that the rest of the party should return by car, but decided that they would return as they came. Never did I regret more that where Churchill went, I had to go also. Wearily I dragged myself round to the camels and asked the Camel Corps sergeant to let me have the quietest and most docile beast there. He agreed, but, thinking himself something of a humorist, he gave me an animal that started off almost before I was in the saddle and raced its way back to the Pyramids without any guidance or consultation with me. How I kept on I do not know. Neither do I know how I should have stopped the camel if the security position had demanded it.

Winston Churchill made no comment at all upon my ride until I was getting back into his car – a painful experience. Then he leaned forward and said, "Well done, Thompson. You're sprightly today. I've not seen you jump about like this for a long time."

PAINTING THE PYRAMIDS

IN EGYPT in 1921 Winston decided that he would like to paint a picture of the Pyramids.

He and I set off together and soon he was settled happily at this task. A small group of British tommies gathered at his back and watched him at work. Even though they were somewhat free with their remarks, I saw no reason to move them on, particularly as Winston appeared to be quietly enjoying their conversation.

Suddenly a young Cockney called out, "You don't half use some paint. Lucky for you, you ain't an 'ouse painter with me old boss. You'd soon get the sack."

Winston chuckled and looked round. The lad got the shock of his life. "Gawd! It's Churchill," he burst out. This was followed by an embarrassed silence. Winston finished what he was doing, and then got off his stool and talked to the boys about their homes and their families for some considerable time.

He gained their confidence and, before he returned to his easel, everyone had a memorable experience to write home about.

I never saw the great man more entertaining, more human or more interested than he was that morning with a group of private British soldiers, far from home, talking to him with open hearts of simple things.

Only Turkish Cigarettes

Mr. churchill himself enjoys a cigar, but there was a time when he did his best to turn me into a non-smoker. In 1921, when I first joined him, I was a heavy pipe smoker and I enjoyed smoking strong brands.

We were on our way to Egypt and Palestine, and I had not quite made up my mind whether I liked being with Mr. Churchill or not. I stood in the corridor of the Blue Train as we ran down towards the Mediterranean Sea, smoking a pipe before breakfast as I contentedly looked out on the beautiful countryside that was all new to me.

My complacency was shaken when Mr. Beckenham, Mr. Churchill's secretary, came out of a compartment and through the open door Winston saw what I was at. He called sharply, "Put that horrible pipe out! The smell is bad – especially at this time of the morning."

After I had done so, I approached him with some trepidation and asked what I was to smoke, only to get the reply, "Only Turkish cigarettes."

I did not like cigarettes at all, especially Turkish ones, and a good deal of my time was spent devising secret methods of smoking my pipe. In effect, I had little time in these conditions to smoke at all.

Later, within a few months, I found that Mr. Churchill took no notice if I smoked Virginian cigarettes, and his tastes must have changed before the last war came, for then he sat round a table with Chiefs of Staff, many of whom, especially the naval representatives, did smoke perfectly foul pipes.

IN THE HIGHLANDS

I KNOW of only one occasion upon which the British Cabinet met in Inverness. It was during the late summer of 1921. Mr. Lloyd George, the then Prime Minister, was fishing in the Highlands and, as several other Ministers were in Scotland, he decided that it was more convenient to ask them to meet him in the ancient Highland capital rather than to ask them to return to London. The Irish troubles were at their height, and the meeting was of some considerable urgency.

When the summons came to go to Inverness, I was with Mr. Churchill, who was staying with his friend, the Duke of Westminster, at Loch More. We had eight hours in which to make the journey, but no means of doing so. The rain had been coming down in sheets for days and the roads, never good at the best of times, were in a deplorable condition.

A car-hirer at Lairg was persuaded to attempt the journey. I confess that when I saw the car my heart went into my mouth. It had certainly seen better days.

All went well for a time and then suddenly the car swerved off the road, bumped down a slope, and came to a stop just short of the edge of a loch. Mr. Churchill made to get out, but hurriedly returned when he found that his boots were ankle deep in mud. Then followed a conference. The driver was quite unconcerned and took the view that we must wait until a passer-by was willing to fetch some horses to tow us out.

Winston got more and more agitated, and eventually persuaded the driver that we might achieve something with the jack. The three of us worked hard with it for an hour and we also collected stones to supplement our efforts.

All this time there was no sign of the passer-by who was to assist us. The only thing that passed was a Royal Mail van and the driver took no notice at all of our efforts to stop him beyond shouting something about "His Majesty's Mails".

Eventually we got the car moving and had time to take stock of ourselves. When we did so, we realised why the postman had been so uncooperative. We looked like three tramps. Our clothes were covered with mud and our hands and faces were filthy. The driver was still philosophical, and seemed to regard the whole proceedings as part of a normal day's motoring in the Highlands more than thirty years ago.

When we were more than half-way to Inverness, the driver suddenly began to take seriously Mr. Churchill's grumbles about the poor speed we were making. He drove like a man possessed along the narrow roads, hurtling us round hair-pin bends and blind corners with no more than a quick touch of his horn. It was a mercy that we met nothing coming the other way. I thought that the old car was going to fall to pieces and would not have been much more uncomfortable if it had, with the rain pouring in through the canvas hood.

We arrived in Inverness just on time. Mr. Churchill was unable to change, and it is certain that no more disreputable-looking figure ever sat down at a meeting of the Cabinet in this country.

Tommy mentions that the "Irish troubles were at their height". Earlier that year he had spotted two Sinn Fein men waiting for Churchill in Hyde Park and prevented Churchill from jumping out of the car with his gun to confront them.

SINN FEIN

FOLLOWING upon the assassination of Sir Henry Wilson outside his home in Eaton Square, Scotland Yard took extraordinary precautions to prevent other British statesmen from becoming the victims of a similar outrage.

For some weeks Churchill lived like a prisoner in a fortress. I was the senior officer responsible for his safety, and it was a nerve-racking time. Plain clothes men patrolled Sussex Square day and night and, when we went out, it was in an armoured Rolls-Royce which Sir John French had used during the war. The car was preceded and followed by Special Branch men, expert marksmen, on motorcycles.

Sinn Fein meant business and our lives were in danger all the time.

I was alarmed one day when Mr. Churchill said to me that he proposed to walk across from the Colonial Office to the House of Commons. I pointed out to him the dangers of this procedure, particularly as there was no other competent person available to go with him at the time.

My remarks had no effect at all. Mr. Churchill just shot out his chin in that obstinate way of his, and replied, "Righto, you look after my back, Thompson. I'll attend to the front."

We reached the House without mishap, but even now I can feel my hand gripping my revolver all the way.

Defeat at Dundee

WHEN the General Election came in 1922, Mr. Churchill was just recovering from an operation for appendicitis. He was really not fit to campaign at all, but he insisted upon going up to his constituency in Dundee for the last week of the election.

His meetings were rowdy, and it was clear to me that he would be hard put to hold his seat. The basic industry in the division was jute and the Depression had already hit jute. Unemployment was rife, and there was a great deal of resentment that the Coalition, of which Churchill had been a member, had not done more for the town.

Dundee was one of the old two-membered constituencies and Winston was running in double harness with Mr. D. L. Macdonald, another Liberal supporter of the Coalition. They were opposed by a mixed bag of candidates consisting of a Prohibitionist, a Socialist, an Independent Liberal and Mr. William Gallacher.

The result was sensational. The Prohibitionist, Mr. Edwin Scrymgeour, topped the poll with 32,588 votes, and the other seat went to the Socialist. Churchill could muster only 20,466 and finished fourth some two thousand votes behind Mr. Macdonald.

It was a bitter blow for a sick man; he was not even well enough to attend the declaration. How well he took it, however! I shall never forget the brave way in which he said to me, "Well, Thompson, that's that. *They* don't want me. I'll have to try elsewhere."

DEFEAT AT LEICESTER

AFTER the election of 1922, the Liberal party reunited on the Free Trade issue, and Mr. Churchill conceived it as his duty to give an anti-socialist lead within the party.

Although easier opportunities were offered to him, he determined to attack the Socialists in one of their own strongholds. The general election of 1923 found him as Liberal candidate in the West division of Leicester. He might have won the seat if the Conservatives had allowed him a straight fight, but at the last minute they threw a third candidate into the field who, while he finished well at the bottom of the poll, obtained more than twice the number of votes that comprised the majority of Mr. F. W. Pethick-Lawrence, the successful Labour nominee.

The Leicester election marked the end of a road for Mr. Churchill. It was quite clear to those closest to him that he had come to regard Socialism as the main enemy, and this was the last occasion upon which he stood as a Liberal, although he was not ready yet to declare himself as a Conservative.

The defeat at Leicester upset Winston far more than his experience at Dundee. He was beginning to wonder what his parliamentary future might be. Just after this election he said to me one day, "It's difficult, after one has been in the House of Commons for a quarter of a century, to realise that one has no longer any right there."

AFTER his successive reverses at Dundee and Leicester, Winston was an unhappy man. He felt keenly his absence from the House of Commons. The chances of his reelection seemed remote, for he had left the Liberal party and could not bring himself to join the Conservatives. The first Labour Government was in office and Churchill was extremely critical of its administration.

In March 1924 a by-election occurred in the Abbey division of Westminster, due to the death of Brig.-Gen. J. S. Nicholson. Winston saw his chance, and with a bold and typically Churchillian gesture announced his intention of contesting the vacancy as an independent Constitutionalist. This move threw both the Conservative and the Liberal camps in the Abbey constituency into confusion.

In the course of my duties, I have witnessed many elections, but this one was quite the most noisy and the most exciting. In addition to Conservative and Liberal candidates, the Socialists selected Mr. A. Fenner Brockway to fight the seat.

Feeling ran very high. The whole Conservative machine was thrown into action to ensure the election of the official candidate, Mr. Otto Nicholson. Churchill was dependent upon the support of only a few personal friends and of the organisation he was able to improvise during the short campaign. Meetings were rowdy, and several fights broke out in the staid streets of Westminster, during one of which the most loyal Churchillian of all, Mr. Brendan Bracken, was stabbed.

By the end of the election, those responsible for Churchill's organisation took a gloomy view of his prospects. They were convinced that the party machines had been too much for him and that he had little chance. So despondent were they that they did not even bother to collect some electors living well outside the constituency who had pledged their support if transport was provided.

I watched the count from the gallery of the Caxton Hall on the night of 19th March 1924. It was an exciting and a memorable occasion. As the votes were counted, it became clear that Nicholson and Churchill had polled nearly the same number of votes, and that Brockway was not far behind. At last the result was ready. Churchill's friends swarmed round him in congratulation as it appeared that he was elected, only to move back as Nicholson's agent demanded a recount.

It was no part of my duty to take sides in the contest, but I should have been less than human if I had not been a Churchill partisan as the recount progressed. I knew how much this meant to him and could feel and share his anxiety. The recount was a bitter disappointment. Nicholson was in, and in spite of a further recount demanded by Churchill's agent, the result remained the same. Conservative majority – 43!

Winston had a cheerful word for his supporters as he left the Caxton Hall, but once he was back in his car being driven away from the scene of near triumph, he slumped into a corner and stared glassily out of the window. It looked as though his bad luck would never end.

Victory at Epping

CHURCHILL did not fight the Abbey division in vain at the famous by-election. Within six months the country was plunged into its third General Election within three years and this time the Conservative party realised at last that it could no longer afford to do without the assistance of its most distinguished ally in the fight against Socialism.

There was a good deal of negotiation before the announcement was made to the public that Mr. Winston Churchill was to contest the Epping division of Essex as a Constitutionalist *with Conservative support.* Epping was a safe Tory seat. It was within easy reach of London and was the ideal constituency for Winston. After three desperate elections, the contest in this pleasant London suburb was like a picnic and Mr. Churchill was returned with a clear majority of 6,000 over the combined votes of his Liberal and Labour opponents. From Winston's point of view, a particularly satisfactory feature was that the Labour candidate lost his deposit.

I have rarely seen him in higher spirits than that day, back at Westerham, when he returned home, Winston Churchill M.P. – again.

His happy association with Epping has continued ever since. Until 1945 he continued to represent the seat with adequate majorities, and when the constituency was divided by the Representation of the People Act of that year, he was elected for the half of the constituency that became known as the Woodford division of Essex.

Chancellor of the Exchequer

As chancellor, Winston was in his element on Budget Day. The air of tension and expectation excited him. Normally he would let me carry his documents for him as we walked over to the House of Commons, but not on Budget Days. Once I asked him if he would like me to carry the little dispatch box for him but he would have none of it.

"No, Thompson," he replied. "There's only one proper person to guard this box: that is me. You guard me."

As Chancellor some of his tussles with Snowden, the Socialist financial expert, provided much of the great House of Commons debating of our time. Churchill revelled in the job as though he knew that it was the prelude to that long, dreary period when he would be out of office when the country needed his great gifts and magnificent capacity for leadership so sorely.

STERLING HONESTY

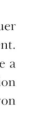

Mr. CHURCHILL was Chancellor of the Exchequer from 1924 to 1929 in the Baldwin Government. One of the fiscal measures he introduced was to place a duty on the import of foreign artificial silk, an action quite obviously in the interests of our own rayon manufactures.

Soon afterwards we attended a meeting at the conclusion of which the Chancellor was presented unexpectedly with two magnificent rayon dressing-gowns, one for Mrs. Churchill and one for himself. They were given by the trade as a token appreciation of the help he had rendered to it.

Immediately, Mr. Churchill sensed the implications of the proposed gift. He thanked the donors for their kind thought, but said, "I cannot take a personal present as a tribute for what I have done in my public capacity. I should like the dressing-gowns, but you must let me pay for them."

There and then he wrote out a cheque for the amount due, which was subsequently handed over to charity.

Nobody would have thought the worse of Mr. Churchill for accepting the presentation, but the idea offended his very high standard of private conduct in public life. He wanted no publicity for his refusal and determined in an instant to deal with the matter firmly, but in the most gracious manner possible.

"I Should Have Been More Careful"

IN RECENT years Mr. Churchill has not driven a car, but there was a time when motoring gave him considerable pleasure. When he was Chancellor of the Exchequer, he often used to drive his modest two-seater from London down to Chartwell.

One Friday, after the House had risen, we were proceeding through the side streets of Croydon, having been directed that way as the main road was under repair, when, as we approached a quite narrow turning to the right, a policeman on duty at the corner signalled us to stop. He did so to enable a bus to turn out of the narrow street towards us.

Instead of pulling up, Mr. Churchill pulled over to his near-side and partly mounted the kerb to enable the bus to pass, which it just succeeded in doing. Winston then started to move off again, but he had reckoned without the constable, who darted behind the bus and stopped us as he was perfectly entitled to do. As a police officer myself I was then startled by the violence of the expressions of this policeman. He abused Mr. Churchill roundly and employed some very objectionable language.

Mr. Churchill listened patiently with his head down, but when the tirade finished, he stuck out his jaw and replied savagely, "Constable, if I have done wrong, you have your remedy, but you have absolutely no right to talk to me like that. Please take his number, Thompson."

As I did so the policeman realised to whom he had been speaking. He appeared horrorstruck, and had the grace to salute before he turned on his heel and walked off disconsolately.

We proceeded on in silence until we came to the outskirts of Westerham, and I heard Winston muttering to himself, "He was right. Yes, he was right. I should have been more careful."

I did not quite know what to make of this so I asked tentatively, "Were you speaking to me, sir?"

Mr. Churchill then replied, "I deserved all he said, you know, although there was no need for him to be so violent about it. I should have paid more attention. Forget all about it, Thompson."

Nothing more was ever said of this incident.

Building His Speeches

THOSE who have listened to the matchless oratory of Mr. Churchill will not always have realised the immense amount of careful and detailed work that goes into the preparation of his speeches. He is a master of repartee and is never at a loss for an answer, either in the House of Commons or in the country. Nevertheless, he takes a great deal more trouble about his set speeches than do many politicians who are able to speak extempore with considerably more effort.

When he is composing a speech for a great occasion, the room is tense with drama. He dictates to his secretary and acts each sentence as he utters it.

He may start off with a great flow of eloquence, but as each page comes off the typewriter he wants to know the total number of words that he has spoken and expects to have this information immediately without hesitation.

Sometimes he stops altogether for a time and paces up and down the room muttering to himself. Then he will start again with appropriate gestures and allowing his voice to rise and fall in the way so familiar to all who have heard him.

Winston is an emotional man, and I have seen the tears running down his cheeks as he rehearses a passage which dwells upon some incident of pathos or mention of disaster. On the other hand he will chuckle away to himself as he coins an epigram or scores an effective debating point.

One dictation is not enough. The original typescript is checked and altered and amended until Mr. Churchill is satisfied that the contents of the speech are the best of which he is capable. I have seen a speech retyped many times before he is satisfied with the text. Incidentally, he does not adopt the American habit of having his speeches prepared for him by "ghost" writers.

When the speech satisfies Mr. Churchill, it is put into what he calls "speech form". Paragraphs, sentences, and even phrases are broken up into the exact periods in which they will be delivered when the speech is made.

He inserts on this form "stage directions" to assist himself in obtaining the maximum effect.

Once the speech is ready, that is the speech he delivers. He studies it carefully time and again and deviates neither from the substance nor from the manner of delivery once he is on his feet talking to his audience.

Tommy noted how well Churchill prepared for his speeches and questions in the House of Commons. In *Guard from the Yard* he revealed that the great orator would often ask Tommy and his secretary for comments on his speech. Tommy delivered any criticism tactfully and it was always well received.

Mary Shearburn, Churchill's secretary and later to be Tommy's second wife, once fell asleep for a few seconds during a period of long dictation late into the night. Tommy noticed and stepped in before Churchill could berate her, asking if he could escort her to her bedroom. Churchill's response was, "Yes. I won't need a good copy of that until 8.30 a.m."

THE CHURCHILL HATS

THERE was perhaps a time when Mr. Churchill took pride in the variety and the eccentricity of his headgear. The cartoonists would certainly have us believe that it was so. During the time I was with him, this was certainly not so. He owned very few hats, although he was inclined to punch those that he did have into any kind of shape that suited his whim of the moment and, if he was photographed wearing the same hat several times, he gave the impression that he was wearing different hats. Perhaps to prevent this happening, in recent years Winston Churchill has only worn two types of hats with any regularity.

On formal occasions he wears the old-fashioned silk hat, which is preserved carefully between outings. Generally, however, he wears now the hat peculiar to himself. It is a type of bowler with an exceptionally high crown. He has several of these, which are always kept well-brushed. They cannot be bashed out of shape and suit his round, chubby face. They have the additional advantage of making him appear taller than he is.

Guarding Churchill while he performs his trademark hat trick following his speech to Congress in 1942.

WHEN Mr. Churchill ceased to be Chancellor of the Exchequer in 1929 on the defeat of the Baldwin Government, I ceased for a time to be his bodyguard. Statesmen out of office are not entitled to Scotland Yard protection, although an exception had been made for Churchill during the years 1922–24 when he was out of office and Parliament because of the special dangers of the Irish situation. It was a great grief to me to leave Mr. Churchill, although I was put on to other work of a particularly interesting nature. Winston, too, had been good enough to express great regret that I was leaving him.

In November 1931 I was told at Scotland Yard that I was earmarked for a special assignment. Great was my pleasure when I discovered that it was proposed that I should visit the United States with Mr. Churchill. This was a unique arrangement. Churchill was to pay my expenses while Scotland Yard continued to pay my salary. As far as I know it had never happened before with a British statesman and it has not happened since. Questions were asked in the House of Commons at the time, highly critical of the proceeding.

The reason for my going was that Mr. Churchill had asked Scotland Yard to release me to accompany him on a lecture tour of the United States and Canada because certain Indian terrorist organisations had made threats against his personal safety.

When I visited Mr. Churchill to discuss the arrangements I was highly gratified to see his face light up as he observed, "So you are coming with me, Thompson. I'm more than glad."

When we arrived in New York, I had my first experience of the American press. The ship had not docked, but at dawn one morning my cabin was besieged by a crowd of men and women making a most fearful row. I thought that the Indian terrorists must be at hand!

They were shouting for Mr. Churchill. I stepped out and asked them who they were and what they wanted.

"Newspapermen," they replied, as though that explained everything. "We must see Churchill."

I replied that I was astonished at their behaviour, and told them bluntly that I had no intention at all of letting them interview the British statesman at this ridiculous hour.

This led to further uproar. Eventually, I persuaded them to go into the lounge, and after a decent interval Churchill came down and spoke to them. I could not help contrasting their attitude with that of British pressmen, whom I have almost always found to be sensible and cooperative. Those whom I met that day were by no means the worst representatives of the American press against whom I have protected Mr. Churchill.

ONE evening in December 1931, Mr. Churchill told me that he proposed to call upon the well-known American statesman Mr. Barney Baruch, and said that there was no need for me to accompany him. I usually on this trip took no notice of these instructions, but followed Winston at a distance if he felt that he could do without protection, just to be on the safe side.

I was, however, very tired that day, and it seemed a good opportunity to have an early night so I went to bed. I was not there long before Mrs. Churchill got me up to tell me that her husband was in hospital as the result of being knocked down by a car.

We rushed to Lenox Hill hospital. Mr. Churchill had been guided there from Fifth Avenue, two streets away, where he had been looking for the house of Mr. Baruch. The blood was running down his face, but he had managed to walk the distance. At the hospital he had been received kindly and efficiently, but the receptionist had wondered whether this dusty and blood-bespattered person was a suitable patient for a private institution.

"Can you afford a private doctor?" she asked.

"Oh, yes," was the reply.

The next question was, "What is your name and profession?"

"I am Winston Churchill, a British statesman," responded the patient. Then he collapsed.

When we got to the hospital, it had become clear that an immediate operation was necessary and that Mr. Churchill was very ill indeed. He had been knocked down by a car driven by an unemployed Italian named Mario Constansino.

Churchill's life remained in danger for about a fortnight, but he kept cheerful. I saw him within a few hours of the accident and his first words to me were, "They almost got me that time, Thompson."

Constansino called daily at the hospital and Mrs. Churchill took an early opportunity of having a talk with the distressed young man. When she heard that he was jobless, she offered him a cheque, but he refused with quiet dignity.

Constansino was one of the first people Winston asked to see when he was well enough to receive visitors, and he left the hospital more cheerfully after Mr. Churchill had gone out of his way to be kind to him. The curly-headed, swarthy-faced Italian carried proudly under his arm an autographed copy of Mr. Churchill's book *The Unknown War*.

In the Watches of the Night

My relations with the British press have always been happy, but during the period when Mr. Churchill was in the Lenox Hill hospital I could not help wishing that one newspaper office in London would realise more clearly that time was different in New York from in London.

The second night after Mr. Churchill's accident, I was awakened and told that the news editor of one of the best known of London's newspapers wanted to speak to either Mrs. Churchill or Miss Diana Churchill. I replied that this they certainly could not do, but that a member of Mr. Churchill's staff would speak to them if the matter was really urgent. The call was not pressed.

The same thing happened the next two nights, and then I did get nettled. I gave instructions that if the newspaper telephoned again, the call was to be put straight through to me. Sure enough, through it came.

I then asked if it was part of the routine in their office only to ring people up in the middle of the night. This took the news editor completely by surprise, and he was profuse in his apologies.

When I got round to giving them the information they were seeking, it was information that they could as easily have obtained in any reference book at a public library without the trouble and expense of initiating London-New York telephone calls.

Afraid

Mr. churchill is a man of infinite courage, but once he gave me the impression of being frightened. It was in the Bahamas at Nassau early in 1932. He had gone there to recuperate after his accident in New York. The hotel at which he stayed was on the corner of a main road, and he was still very weak.

One morning we were out for a walk, and as we came out of the hotel a Ford car came round the corner very fast, driven by a coloured man. There was no pavement, and Winston clasped my arm and leaned back against the wall, trembling. His face had gone as white as a sheet and beads of perspiration stood out on his forehead.

I was alarmed at this and said to him, gently, "Sir, you really must not do that. Try to pull yourself together."

I could feel him bracing himself before he replied, "Yes, Thompson, it was silly of me, but it won't occur again."

It never did.

A Note of Warning

During the tense days of August 1939, Miss Mary Shearburn (later to be my wife), in her secretarial capacity, accompanied Mr. and Mrs. Churchill to St. Georges Motel when they stayed at the home of Madame Balsan.

The international situation fluctuated from day to day, and the British and French press alternated between optimism and pessimism about the possibility of war with confusing frequency.

On the outward journey, my wife travelled part of the way in Mr. Churchill's car, taking notes for him. When he had finished his work he lapsed into silence, and she sat looking out of the window at the beautiful and peaceful country through which they were passing. The corn was ripe and, in its heaviness, it looked like the golden waves of a gently undulating sea.

Mr. Churchill grew graver and graver as he sat wrapped in thought, and then said slowly and sorrowfully, "Before the harvest is gathered in, we shall be at war."

3rd September 1939

I HAD emerged from retirement on 22nd August 1939, to take up my old appointment as bodyguard to Mr. Winston Churchill. During a fateful fortnight, I was with him while, still out of office, he waited for the war, which now appeared inevitable, to start. His warnings had gone unheeded. He had tried to point out to the obstinate men who had held power since 1931, first the way in which war might be avoided, and secondly the need for adequate preparation in case war came. His advice and his warnings were consistently ignored. He received nothing but ridicule and cold-shouldering from the politicians in office. The treatment meted out to him would have turned a lesser man sour and bitter.

Then it came. Within a few minutes of Chamberlain's broadcast telling the nation that we were at war with Germany, the air raid sirens sounded over London.

Churchill went outside and stood staring into the sky. What thoughts must have been crowding into his mind at that moment! It was with difficulty that we prevailed upon him to enter an air-raid shelter. He agreed to go only when it was pointed out that it was up to him to set an example.

Down we went into a basement, the Old Man with a bottle of brandy under his arm. There he paced up and down, just as he had done on that day over seventeen years before, when I had my first interview with him.

As soon as the "All Clear" sounded, Churchill rushed up to the roof of Morpeth Mansions where he had his flat, and stood there trying to discern aircraft in the cloudless sky.

Next on that memorable Sunday, we went to the House of Commons, where Churchill with characteristic generosity went out of his way to pay tribute to the good intentions of Mr. Neville Chamberlain in the following words, "In this solemn hour, it is a consolation to recall and to dwell upon our repeated efforts for peace. All have been ill-starred, but all have been faithful and sincere."

When the Commons adjourned he came to me and said briefly, "10 Downing Street, Thompson."

When he returned to the car after his interview with the Prime Minister, he was smiling, and as the door was opened for him he called to Mrs. Churchill, sitting waiting for him, "It's the Admiralty. That's a lot better than I thought."

THE MISSING BOXES

AT THE end of 1939, an incident occurred that upset me greatly and brought down upon my head the just wrath of Mr. Churchill.

He had been staying with Lord and Lady Digby at Cerne Abbas after inspecting naval establishments at Weymouth. On the return journey by train, I was in charge of two boxes of official papers as well as of Mr. Churchill. I gave priority to Mr. Churchill and put the boxes down with the rest of the luggage. I did not want to leave the First Lord, as there were a good many strangers about on the platform.

I accompanied Mr. Churchill to his compartment, and was diverted by the arrival of a third box of papers by special messenger from London. Before the train left I enquired if the two boxes were aboard, and I was assured that they were.

When I returned to the compartment, I looked for the boxes and could not find them. The train was moving very fast by this time, and by the time I had checked the position with the valet, the messenger from London and Miss Mary Shearburn, Mr. Churchill's secretary, we had crossed the points and were out on the main lines.

I got the train stopped at the next station – Churchill sitting as stiffly and grimly as I have ever seen him all the

way, but saying nothing – and telephoned back to see if the boxes were safe. I found that the stationmaster had them in safe custody, and was that much relieved.

Then the storm broke. The Old Man gave me a first-class dressing-down and I could only agree that I had been careless. I was willing to take the whole blame.

He then sent for Miss Shearburn and addressed her in similar terms. She was no less upset, but bravely agreed that the fault lay with her.

Mr. Churchill saw that we were both trying to shield each other and this brought out his essential kindliness. His face was still stern, but there was a twinkle in his eyes as he finished, "You had *both* better be more careful in future."

I am not sure that he did not guess the reason why we were trying to lift the blame from each other's shoulders. I later married Miss Shearburn.

Within a day or two, Winston cheered me up by going out of his way to tell me how much he appreciated the careful way in which I looked after his possessions, and closed the interview by saying, "I am sure the lapse was not entirely your fault."

AT SCAPA FLOW

WHEN, in December 1939, a German U-boat penetrated the defences at Scapa Flow and sunk the battleship *Royal Oak,* Mr. Churchill allowed himself to show something of the chagrin that he felt. I heard him say quietly to himself, "If only they had taken notice of me a few years ago, this would not have happened."

We had been to Scapa Flow a few weeks before and, strangely enough, as we passed through the boom defences I had asked Mr. Churchill whether there was any possibility of a U-boat following us in before the boom closed.

When the disaster occurred I remembered the extremely general way in which he had answered me. "*I hope* they will not be able to do so. According to the powers-that-be, who give me information on this subject, the possibility of U-boats entering is very remote."

He was obviously not happy about the position and, in spite of the sinking being one of the most brilliant naval exploits of the war, on either side, it should not have happened.

WHEN, in 1939, Mr. Churchill, as First Lord of the Admiralty, was going to visit the Fleet at Scapa Flow, Miss Mary Shearburn accompanied us on part of the journey north. It was arranged that she should get off the train at Carlisle at midnight and catch the 2 a.m. train back to London.

As we began to approach the Scottish border, Mr. Churchill explained to her that a police escort had been arranged for her at Carlisle station, as she would be carrying the box containing the official papers on which they had been working during the journey. He added, however, that once she began the return journey, she would be in a sleeping-compartment by herself and would be solely responsible for the safe custody of the box. He asked, "In the event of anyone attacking you to get the box, what would you do?"

The First Lord looked a little surprised when she replied, "I would scream at the top of my voice."

She then added, "You know it is the best way of discouraging unwelcome attentions of any sort. It attracts so much publicity."

Winston grinned and nodded his head, adding, "You may well be right. I should never have thought of it."

The Cameraman

MR. CHURCHILL did not always respect the rules created for his own protection. One of my duties was to ensure that photographs were not taken of him with landmarks in the background that could be recognised.

While he was at the Admiralty, we were walking over one day to 10 Downing Street when a press photographer intercepted us. This was not a suitable place for a photograph and I waved the pressman aside.

Winston, however, had other ideas. He called to the cameraman, "Do you want to take a photograph?"

"Yes, please, sir," was the reply.

The photograph was taken and I was not pleased. I turned to Churchill and said, "I thought that photographs were forbidden here, sir?"

"Ah, well," came the answer, with that irresistible boyish grin. "After all, he is one of God's children, Thompson."

But then he saw that I was not mollified, and in the garden of No. 10 he returned to the subject. "They have to do something to get a little copy, you know."

FROM September 1939 to May 1940, Mr. Neville Chamberlain remained as War Prime Minister. There was a great deal of agitation in the country to remove him from this position and to have Winston Churchill appointed in his stead. Churchill never gave any encouragement to those who desired this change, and, indeed, throughout the debate on the fall of Norway that brought about the fall of the Chamberlain Government he gave complete and loyal support to the Prime Minister.

The need, however, was for Coalition, but the leaders of the other parties refused to serve with Chamberlain, whom they regarded as the architect of disaster. He hung on to office as long as he could, but on 10th May 1940 he had to bow to the inevitable. He resigned and His Majesty the King called upon Winston Spencer Churchill, the only possible choice, to form a government.

When we came back from Buckingham Palace to the Admiralty – a journey that was made in complete silence – the new Prime Minister, as he was getting out of the car, without warning, said to me, "You know why I have been to Buckingham Palace, Thompson?"

I replied, "Yes, sir. May I say how pleased I am that you have at last become Prime Minister? I only wish that the position had come your way in better times, for you have taken on an enormous task."

Tears came into his eyes as he answered gravely, "God alone knows how great it is. I hope that it is not too late. I am very much afraid that it is. We can only do our best."

That was all I heard. As he turned away he muttered something to himself. Then he set his jaw and with a look of determination, mastering all emotion, he began to climb the stairs of the Admiralty.

It was the greatest privilege of my life to have shared those few moments with him.

The Famous Cigars

MR. CHURCHILL does not smoke as many cigars as he is reputed to do.

He likes to smoke a cigar, but he realises that the public like to see him doing so even more. He, therefore, takes good care to ensure that a cigar is in his mouth on all special occasions!

When at work, however, he will often let his cigar go out and will chew the cigar for a long time before he relights it. He sometimes makes the same cigar last several hours in this way.

He smokes only the best, and in recent years he has not had to buy many of these. Admirers all over the world have been only too pleased to provide him with an almost embarrassing abundance of cigars as a token of their admiration for all that he has accomplished.

Churchill's preferred cigar lighter.

THE WHISTLING BOY

WINSTON Churchill, Prime Minister of Great Britain, was walking along King Charles Street to Downing Street during the war.

Approaching him from the other direction was a young boy of about fifteen, hands in pockets, whistling loudly and cheerfully.

Mr. Churchill cannot stand whistling, and as the boy came near called to him in a sharp, stern voice, "Stop that whistling!"

The boy looked up at the Prime Minister with complete unconcern and answered, "Why should I?"

"Because I don't like it, and it's a horrible noise," growled Churchill.

The boy strolled on, and then turned to call out, "Well, you can shut your ears, can't you?"

And with that he resumed whistling at full blast. Mr. Churchill was completely taken aback and, for a moment, looked furious. Then, as we crossed the road into the Foreign Office yard, he began to smile. Quietly he repeated to himself the words "You can shut your ears, can't you?" and followed them with one of his famous chuckles.

I<small>T WAS</small> just after Germany had attacked through the Low Countries in May 1940. The newspapers were full of optimism as was the Prime Minister, Mr. Neville Chamberlain.

A meeting took place of the Supreme War Council. Chamberlain was present with Daladier, the French Prime Minister, who said it was the finest war council he had ever attended. I stood at the side of the group and watched the statesmen and the officials having their photographs taken.

Back at the British Embassy, Mr. Churchill suddenly asked me, "Did you have your picture taken with the group, Thompson?"

"No, sir."

"Pity. I am certain that the people in that group will never meet again in similar circumstances."

Within a few weeks Daladier was a prisoner of the Germans and Chamberlain had been replaced as Prime Minister by Churchill himself.

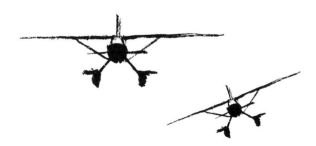

SLEEPING UNDERGROUND

DURING the war hundreds of thousands of Londoners used the underground stations as air-raid shelters at night. So did Mr. Churchill. The disused Down Street tube station was fitted up as a special shelter for Mr. Churchill and his colleagues. The Prime Minister disliked intensely being confined in this way, and great pressure had to be used by many influential people to persuade him that it was of vital importance that he took no unnecessary risks.

Later it was possible to construct alternative shelter accommodation at the Annexe to No. 10 Downing Street. Winston went below, when he did go, with the greatest reluctance and much preferred to continue working through the air raids at ground level. This worried Mrs. Churchill and members of the Cabinet.

One evening Mrs. Churchill, before she left him, extracted a promise that he would go below if a raid took place. She informed me that she hoped I would ensure that he did so.

As soon as news that a raid was pending arrived, I informed the Prime Minister. He gathered up his papers and proceeded to the basement in an exemplary manner. I was mystified by this unusual docility and somewhat apprehensive when I noticed the mysterious smile on his face.

He got into bed, and as I left the room, I made to turn off the light.

"Leave it on, Thompson," said the Old Man.

I sat in my room and within a few minutes the bell rang.

When I went to the Prime Minister's room, I found him out of bed in his dressing-gown, with a stack of papers under his arm. I looked at him in surprise, and a mischievous grin spread all over his face.

"Well, Thompson," said he. "I have kept my word. I came downstairs to go to bed. Now I am going upstairs to work."

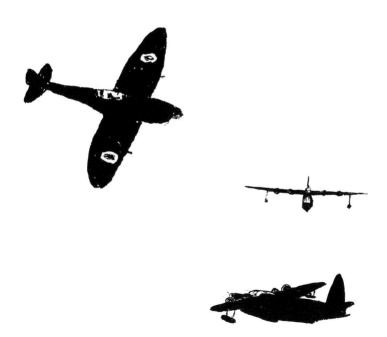

DUNKIRK

WHEN the fall of France appeared imminent in 1940, I flew with Mr. Churchill to Paris for consultations with M. Reynaud and other French Ministers. Although it was not generally realised at the time, the object of these discussions was to persuade the French Government to carry on the war against Hitler's Germany even if the struggle had to be abandoned in metropolitan France.

As we flew over stricken France, I could see from the plane hordes of refugees, carrying what they could, flying in panic before the mechanised might of the German Army. Mr. Churchill's face was drawn and grey, and his only topic of conversation was upon the possibility of getting back at least some of the British Expeditionary Force to England through Dunkirk.

In Paris the bargaining with the French Government was hard, for it was permeated with a spirit of defeatism and worse. Churchill was working hard upon them and Reynaud was giving him what assistance he could in the face of his own incredibly difficult personal position. Everywhere I went in the French capital I heard different and alarming stories about the fate of the French Army and the B.E.F.

I was as despondent as anyone, although, like a true Englishman, the thought of ultimate defeat in the war never crossed my mind until one evening as he was going into dinner the Prime Minister turned to me and said, "Thompson, how many men do you think we have evacuated from Dunkirk?"

I replied, "I am afraid I cannot guess, sir, as I do not know the number of troops we had in Belgium."

"But you must have a guess," he insisted.

I could see that his face was a little more cheerful as I suggested, "Fifty thousand, sir?"

"Thompson," said the Prime Minister, "I thought we should be lucky if we got away safely twenty thousand, but now, thank God, ninety thousand are already back in England, and we hope for many more to come."

Four-fifths of the B.E.F. and several thousands of French troops were brought safely back to England. The Prime Minister was like a man with a great load lifted from his back.

Tommy later described how they had almost been shot down on one of the trips across to France. Churchill commented, "That pilot did not know how close he came to getting the Iron Cross, first class!"

"THE SAME CHANCE AS THE REST"

SOMETIMES during the bombing Mr. Churchill seemed to be quite reckless. Once we stood on the roof of the No. 10 Annexe watching the German bombers attacking London. Suddenly Winston said quietly and sincerely, "When my time is due, it will come."

Another day we visited a gun-site in Richmond Park. We travelled in an armoured car.

As we left the Park, he noticed that the officers accompanying him were getting into ordinary staff cars. Once he saw this nothing could persuade him to get into the armoured car again. In the saloon he remarked firmly, "I must take the same chance as the rest."

Testing a Sten gun.
Churchill often inspected the army's weaponry.

DURING the Blitz it was quite impossible to keep the Prime Minister in an air-raid shelter for any length of time. Mrs. Churchill and his colleagues in the Government reasoned with him on this matter many times and it was possible to get him down into the shelters sometimes. To keep him there was another matter. He was restless all the time and at the slightest excuse would be outside looking at the raiders and finding out what was going on in the immediate vicinity.

One night during a raid, he and Sir John Anderson stood in the doorway of the No. 10 Annexe watching the searchlights picking out the raiders. I got more and more alarmed for their safety as we could hear bombs dropping fairly close.

I heard a whistling through the air, and in a second I had my arms around Mr. Churchill and flung him with all my strength behind the door.

He was horrified and indignant. "Don't do that!" he roared at me.

In a few minutes he recovered his composure, and he must have realised that there was sense in what I had done for shrapnel was flying about and a colleague of mine who was with us at the time was hit.

This was one of the times when my training as a police athlete came in useful. Mr. Churchill is not built to be flung through the air.

A Hard Driver

Working for Mr. Winston Churchill, particularly in wartime, involved long hours and required great stamina and powers of endurance.

At one of the most critical moments of the war, just after he became Prime Minister, we returned from Paris. Lord Halifax was with us. At Hendon, Churchill turned to him and said, "We will have a Cabinet meeting at ten o'clock tonight."

Lord Halifax did not seem very pleased, and he pleaded, "We have had rather a long and tiring day, Winston. Cannot the Cabinet be held tomorrow morning?"

Mr. Churchill made him a concession. "Oh, yes. All right, we'll have the Cabinet at half-past ten tonight instead."

THE arrangement throughout the war was that a Scotland Yard detective should always be with Mr. Churchill to ensure that he was never out without police protection. Generally, this worked admirably, but on one occasion the arrangement broke down.

Whenever Mr. Churchill had his lunch, I took the opportunity to have mine. This day he was at 10 Downing Street, and when he went into lunch I went out to a café at Oxford Circus, leaving a colleague in charge. As I came out I was surprised to see the police car that should have been standing by at No. 10 proceeding down Oxford Street at a great pace. I knew that the car should not leave Downing Street without accompanying the Prime Minister, and in great alarm I commandeered a taxi – they were not always easy to get by normal methods in those days – and made my way back as fast as possible.

When I arrived I found that my colleague had thought it safe to go over to nearby New Scotland Yard, to make an enquiry, and that he had been detained there longer than he had anticipated. When he got back the Prime Minister had gone. He set off in pursuit.

Long before Mr. Churchill got back I was on the pavement outside No. 10 looking for him. At last he drove back quite safely, accompanied by Commander Thompson, the Arrangements Secretary. On seeing me the Prime Minister made a remark to Commander Thompson, and they both laughed heartily.

As Mr. Churchill got out of the car, he called to me,

with a mischievous grin on his face, "I got away from you that time, Thompson."

To this, I replied, "Not from me, sir. I lunch when you do. My colleague should have been here."

Seeing that I was still obviously upset, Winston added, "Never mind, Thompson. It was a sudden call to see Mr. Hopkins off from Hendon, and I am back safe and sound."

When Commander Thompson joined me later, he was still amused, and remarked, "As soon as Mr. Churchill saw you waiting for him he turned to me and said, "I bet Thompson is mad because I got away without him."

Churchill did not often let Tommy leave his side; rare exceptions were the few occasions when he accompanied doubles of Churchill. Doubles of Tommy were harder to find, as he was a distinctive-looking man and tall for his era.

The Churchill Tanks

MR. CHURCHILL took great pride in the tank named after him and did not relish much the criticism of them made by Mr. R. R. Stokes and others in the House of Commons.

In 1942, soon after the fall of Singapore, he determined to see if there was anything amiss himself. Reports showed that the gear boxes were giving trouble, and he asked that a large-scale test should be arranged.

This took place on the Sussex Downs, and seventy or eighty tanks were employed. The testing-ground was a difficult one and, for a time, the tanks were on their best behaviour. Then one or two started to ease up, but, before the Prime Minister could get over to them, they were off again.

An officer standing by me said, "Of course, it would happen like this today. The tanks are all right, but the gearboxes are always giving trouble. They are not strong enough."

Mr. Churchill inspected the tanks after the trials, and just when those in charge thought that he had finished, he started to put searching questions to some of the drivers. The soldiers spoke up without inhibitions and it was not long before, from the information given, the root of the trouble was diagnosed.

O N A tour of the South Coast, the Mayor of Ramsgate asked Mr. Churchill to accompany him into the famous chalk shelters. This was when the Battle of Britain was at its height during the summer of 1940.

As we went in a man asked Winston for a cigar jokingly, and much, I am sure, to his surprise received one.

An alert had been sounded as the Prime Minister stood with the Mayor just inside the entrance to the shelter. He was approached by a newsboy calling the local evening paper. Now Winston can never resist buying a newspaper. He delights in reading them, although I should have thought that he would have found much in them something of a bore, in view of his opportunities for garnering more accurate information elsewhere. I was, therefore, surprised when he took no notice of the boy.

When the boy looked as though he was becoming a considerable nuisance with his persistent "Please buy a paper from me", I told him off, somewhat impatiently.

As I did so, the Premier suddenly realised that he was there and what he wanted. Out came a two-shilling piece, a paper was produced, and the one and eleven pence change was waved airily aside.

"THOMPSON HAS GUARDED ME FAITHFULLY"

DURING the Atlantic Meeting of August 1941, I accompanied Mr. Churchill over to the *Augusta*, where he was to have dinner with President Roosevelt. Talking to my opposite number Mike Reilly of the American F.B.I., I expressed an ambition to meet Mr. Roosevelt. He said that he would arrange for me to be introduced to the President that evening.

We were on the way to arrange this when we met Mr. Churchill. I explained to him what we had in mind, and he replied, "Oh, no. I will perform that introduction myself."

He turned round, led me into the cabin, and said to Mr. Roosevelt, "Inspector Thompson has guarded me faithfully for a period of nearly twenty years. It gives me great pleasure to present him to you."

It was a proud moment.

The President talked for a few minutes and as he said goodbye, added, "Look after the Prime Minister. He is one of the greatest men in the world."

Roosevelt also enquired about Churchill's habits of work and rest and whether Tommy found him "troublesome".

Shoulder to shoulder with President Roosevelt's bodyguards.

CHRISTMAS 1941 found us staying at the White House, Washington. The United States was now in the war and the Prime Minister had much to discuss with the President. In the midst of their preoccupation with the war, I was touched on Christmas Day to receive a small package which, when I opened it, I found to contain a very nice tie with the message, "Christmas 1941 – A Merry Christmas from the President and Mrs. Roosevelt."

It was on this visit that Mr. Churchill spoke in the Canadian House of Commons, and I was glad to be there when the Prime Minister made a famous remark. Speaking of France he said, "But their chiefs misled them. When I warned them that Britain would fight on alone, their chiefs told their Prime Minister that in three weeks England would have her neck wrung like a chicken. SOME CHICKEN! SOME NECK!"

When the business was concluded in Ottawa and Washington, it was decided that Mr. Churchill would be the better for a rest before he returned to bomb-weary Britain. We, therefore, flew down to a villa at Palm Beach. The Old Man's idea of a holiday was somewhat peculiar. He took an hour or two off each day, but continued to work until the small hours each morning.

Soon after he arrived Mr. Churchill told me that he would like to do some swimming while he was at Palm Beach and requested me to make the necessary arrangements. I asked him if he had a swimming-suit, or would he like me to obtain one for him.

His reply startled me.

"I don't think I need one," said he. "It is entirely private here. Nobody knows I am staying at this place and I have only to step out of the back door into the sea."

"You could be seen through glasses, sir," I suggested.

"If they are that much interested, it is their own fault what they see," growled Winston.

So it was. We did compromise with him by getting him to use a large towel, which he was to throw to his valet as he entered the water.

The American newspapers would have given a great deal for a photograph of the British Prime Minister, naked as a baby, swimming strongly in the water and turning over and over like a porpoise.

THE SHARK AT PALM BEACH

DURING Mr. Churchill's holiday at Palm Beach, he decided to have one final bathe before he returned to Washington.

As he got ready a shout from the beach conveyed the information that a fifteen-foot shark had just swum to within a few yards of the shore, but that it was probably a harmless sand shark.

"I am not so sure about that," said Winston with a smile. "I want to see his identity card before I trust myself to him."

As he sat down in the shallows by the water's edge, he asked me to keep a sharp lookout.

"Let me know if that 'inoffensive' shark comes back," he said.

But we saw no more of it, and when he left the water Mr. Churchill remarked, "My bulk must have frightened him away!"

Wɪᴛʜ the single exception of the fall of France, the early part of 1942 was almost certainly the most discouraging period of the whole war for the Allies.

First, the great liner *Normandie* was burnt down to its hulk as it was being prepared for war service. This was followed by the humiliating incident when the German ships *Scharnhorst* and *Gneisenau* steamed up our Channel, unmolested, making many knots, after they had been subjected over a period of many months to concentrated and heavy bombing.

To crown all, Singapore fell. This calamity appalled Churchill. In all my years of working with him, I never saw him so upset about anything. He had placed such faith in this "impregnable bastion" in the Far East. Only six weeks previously I had heard him assure a press conference in Ottawa that Singapore could not be taken.

The news dismayed our Dominions and Colonies. It left Australia wondering where her hope of defence lay.

When friends asked the Prime Minister what had happened at Singapore, he would shake his head dismally and say, "I really don't know."

All the efforts by his intimates and by his staff to take his mind off the disaster failed for a long time.

He stayed one weekend just after the fall of Singapore with Mr. and Mrs. Ronald Tree at Ditchley Park.

He was downcast. He was overtired, exhausted, and sleeping little. He was more worried that I have ever known him. On the Saturday afternoon he was persuaded to go to bed. Realising that rest was essential if the Prime

Minister was to avoid a complete breakdown, strict instructions were given that the house was to be kept completely quiet while he tried to rest.

Within half an hour he sent for me. The telephone had rung in his room, owing to a switch being accidentally moved.

It would have been a relief if this had been made the occasion of a round of Churchillian invective. He was not, however, angry. He was pathetic. He said, in a miserable voice, "Sleep for me is finished. I shall do some work."

I take legitimate pride in the knowledge that it was a suggestion of mine that helped to break this terrible mood of Mr. Churchill. I knew that he took great delight in visiting Service establishments, and I ventured, at the risk of possible wrath, to tell him that I thought he ought to renew these visits. To my relief, after some hesitation, he agreed.

"The Road to Mandalay"

IT WAS at Chequers, just after the Japanese had swept through Burma. There was one of the film shows on that Winston delighted to organise for his guests and the household staff.

We were assembled in the Great Parlour when Mr. Churchill came in. The loud-speaker blared out the tune "The Road to Mandalay".

He was not amused.

"It's a little late for that," said the Premier grimly.

10TH August 1942 was a great day for me. Our plane touched down at an airfield near Moscow and Mr. Churchill stepped out to be greeted by Stalin and Molotov. That same evening he started conferences with Generalissimo Stalin.

They did not always proceed smoothly. Within an hour or two Mr. Churchill was out of the room stalking down the corridor in obvious displeasure. I learnt afterwards that the British Prime Minister had been asked for a decision and that his answer had failed to please Stalin.

For the next two days, the discussions were carried on by the military Chiefs except that all of the British party attended the most lavish State banquet I have ever seen – and I have been at a good many functions of this sort in my time.

After the meal we adjourned to another room where champagne, liqueurs and coffee were served. Mr. Churchill seemed uneasy and he drew Sir Alexander Cadogan aside and talked quietly to him in a corner.

Within a few minutes Sir Alexander told Pavlov, Stalin's interpreter, that Mr. Churchill wished to see Stalin alone. But Stalin would not play. He intended to have a night's enjoyment and no discussions.

Winston had had enough. He jumped up from his seat and called to Cadogan, "Come along, I'm going. Tell the Marshal if he wishes to have any further discussions I shall be at the villa until Sunday morning. Then I am leaving for Cairo as arranged."

When we left the Kremlin, Stalin accompanied us to the entrance.

Later I was told that I was to go with Mr. Churchill to the Kremlin again at 6 p.m. on the Saturday evening. Nobody else came with us, and after the Prime Minister had gone in to see Stalin I was left by myself in the hall. It was a strange feeling to be alone in this seat of mystery more especially as very soon I found myself in the midst of an altercation with two Russian police officials who wanted me to return to the villa. After the argument they became quite pleasant and arranged for me to have some food, while Mr. Churchill dined with the Soviet leader.

The conference did not end until 2 a.m. Sir Alexander Cadogan arrived during the late evening and together we waited for the Prime Minister.

When Mr. Churchill did at last appear, he was in great form and seemed pleased and satisfied with the result of the session.

Tommy later recorded how uncomfortable he felt about not being in the same room as Churchill and not knowing exactly where in the building the meeting was taking place.

A Soldier Gets a Cigar

A FTER the 1942 Moscow Conference, we went to
Cairo, and then the Prime Minister visited troops in
the forward area. The soldiers were both surprised and
delighted to see him. I heard one man shout to his
comrades, "Here's old Winston, b****y hat, umbrella,
cigar and all!"

The keynote of these visits to the fighting troops was
informality, but perhaps it was well that everybody was
not as informal as the private who shouted to the Prime
Minister, "What about a cigar, sir?"

Winston stopped, looked at him, and suddenly said,
"Why not? Of course, you shall have one." He offered the
soldier his case.

Tommy told us that people would fight over Churchill's cigar
wrappers for souvenirs.

GIRAUD AND DE GAULLE

THE Casablanca Conference in January 1943 opened in a difficult atmosphere. The leadership of the Free French Forces presented something of a problem. General de Gaulle had very obvious claims to the premier position, but he was not an easy man to get on with. It is said by those who should know – I cannot vouch for the truth of this – that Mr. Churchill, exasperated beyond measure, on one occasion remarked, "I have many crosses to bear, but the greatest is the Cross of Lorraine."

In any case, it was known that de Gaulle had made so many enemies by his blunt speaking that he was not acceptable in metropolitan France.

The experiment was tried of appointing Admiral Darlan Chief of State, and Leader of the French Empire. This not only infuriated the Gaullists, it also gave rise to a first-class political row in the House of Commons where many members of all parties considered that the record of Darlan was a disgraceful one. This unhappy expedient was abruptly terminated on Christmas Eve when Darlan was assassinated in Algiers.

The strongest candidate for leadership, apart from de Gaulle, was General Giraud, who had a distinguished record as a soldier, and had recently escaped from a German prison camp (a feat that he had previously accomplished during the First World War). Both de Gaulle and Giraud were at Casablanca and I remember Mr. Churchill coming out of a discussion with President Roosevelt well after midnight, and saying to me, "Sorry to keep you out so late, Thompson, but we have to marry these two somehow!"

Next day the Prime Minister had a long conversation with General de Gaulle, who looked far from pleased. Together they started off to President Roosevelt's villa.

Half-way there I saw Mr. Murphy, the President's representative, with General Giraud. De Gaulle saw them, too, and half-turned as though to go back whence he had come.

After an uncomfortable pause the two French soldiers shook hands, albeit half-heartedly, and they all entered President Roosevelt's villa together.

A compromise was patched up satisfactory to General de Gaulle's dignity and the conference was able to devote itself to others matters.

One could not help noticing how much more relaxed Mr. Churchill became after this matter was settled.

WITH THE EIGHTH ARMY

AFTER the Casablanca Conference we visited Turkey and Cyprus, where Mr. Churchill took great pleasure in inspecting his old regiment, the 4th Hussars. Then we went on to Cairo and flew to General Montgomery's headquarters at Tripoli.

When we landed in Tripoli, the Prime Minister was immediately surrounded by R.A.F. personnel, in the centre of whom, struggling towards us, could be seen General Montgomery. Mr. Churchill almost embraced the General in his pleasure at meeting him again.

On Friday 5th February 1943, when we came to the main body of the troops of the historic Eighth Army, they cheered lustily. Later they marched past, and what a march it was!

General Montgomery and the Prime Minister reviewed the troops in the Western Desert after they had fought their way from Alamein, and they looked as though they had just come out of Wellington Barracks. Their vehicles were shining like new. Their boots were polished, their trousers pressed, their equipment clean and their heads held high.

"I really do not know where they got their polish," said General Montgomery.

Mr. Churchill chuckled as he answered, "Trust the British tommy to find some, when required."

Winston is an artist and in Castle Square a sentry caught his artist's eye. He was standing in the archway of what had been a window, fifty feet above the ground. He was silhouetted against the sky, the building behind him having been destroyed by bombs.

115

Came the order from Mr. Churchill, "Stop the car!" He drew everybody's attention to the picture and asked that photographs should be taken and copies sent to him.

It was a moving moment when the Prime Minister spoke to the assembled Eighth Army. It would have needed a heart of stone to miss the emotion. He told them that they reminded him of the words of the well-known hymn, "Each night you pitch your moving tent, a day's march nearer home." In conclusion he said what we all must have felt. "After this war is over, it will be sufficient for you to say when you are asked, 'What did you do?' to reply, 'I marched with the Eighth Army.'"

Two conferences that followed close upon each other were the meetings at Cairo and Teheran. There was some duplication in the business because Generalissimo Chiang Kai-shek and Marshal Stalin did not wish to meet as the Soviet Union was not at war with Japan. Chiang Kai-shek was present at the Cairo Conference, but Stalin was not there; whereas at Teheran the Soviet leader attended, but Chiang Kai-shek was not invited.

The conference at Teheran was held in the Soviet Embassy there, and on the second day a great ceremony took place when Mr. Churchill presented the Stalingrad Sword to Marshal Stalin. It was a most impressive occasion. After a lunch given by the Shah of Persia, I carried the case in which the sword had been transported from England into the Embassy, placing it on a table in the centre of the room.

On one side stood twenty soldiers from the Buffs with rifles and bayonets fixed; on the other, twenty Russian privates with Tommy guns across their chests.

Between the two lines, but slightly in front of our soldiers, stood a British lieutenant with the Sword between his feet.

Mr. Churchill, wearing the uniform of an Air Commodore, arrived just as Marshal Stalin came through the door opposite. President Roosevelt followed Stalin.

The British officer moved forward with the sword held in front of him. Mr. Churchill then said, "Marshal Stalin, I have a command from His Majesty, King George VI, to present you, for transmission to the city of Stalingrad,

In the presence of Roosevelt, Churchill orders
the Stalingrad sword to be presented to Stalin
at the Teheran Conference of 1943.

this sword of honour, the design of which His Majesty himself approved. The blade bears the inscription, 'To the steel-hearted citizens of Stalingrad, a gift from King George VI in token of homage of the British peoples'."

The national anthems of the two countries were then played, and the Premier handed the sword to Marshal Stalin. The Marshal, smiling with pleasure, lifted the sword to his lips and in absolute silence kissed the scabbard.

As he handed the sword to Marshal Voroshilov, Stalin let the blade fall from the scabbard, but he managed to retrieve it quickly.

President Roosevelt expressed a desire to see the sword. When Stalin showed it to him he held it by the hilt and said aloud, "Truly a heart of steel. Yes, the word steel-hearted represents the people of Stalingrad."

What Tommy does not mention is that he had to lug the heavy sword around before it was presented, as well as guard Churchill in this difficult place.

W E FLEW to Tunis after the Teheran Conference. On the journey it became increasingly clear that the Prime Minister was very unwell. As soon as we arrived at the White House in Tunis he went straight to bed, and the news was given out that he had pneumonia.

I volunteered to spend the night with him. At 11 p.m. Lord Moran, his doctor, told me to watch the tempo of Mr. Churchill's breathing and, if there was any sudden alteration, to call him immediately.

I sat outside the door, and I could hear distinctly the Prime Minister's fast, stertorous breathing. About two o'clock in the morning, the sounds ceased.

I opened the door and crept into the bedroom. All was silent. I reached the bedside. Still silence. I was sick in my stomach. I do not remember in my life such a feeling of shock and fear.

I leaned over the bed and brought my head down almost to Winston's pillow. He was breathing quietly and steadily. With a feeling of terrific relief – although it was some hours before I recovered from the first shock – I went to report to Lord Moran.

He came to the bedside, listened and said, "He is breathing better now. You were quite right to call me."

Later the same night I found Mr. Churchill groping about the dressing-table. He was looking for his sleeping tablets. I pretended to help him, although I knew that they had been removed as a precaution. I was relieved when he said, "Oh, it doesn't matter."

He lay back on the pillow and said drearily, "Thompson,

I am tired out in body, soul and spirit."

"Not in spirit, sir," I answered. "You are just tired after a strenuous time. Now that the conferences are ended I hope that you will be able to get a little rest."

After talking for a minute or two, suddenly, he sat up in bed, and flung out his arms, crying, "All is planned and ready. In what better place could I die than here – in the ruins of Carthage?"

He sighed and dropped off to sleep like a little child. It was certainly one of the most remarkable nights in my experience. I was glad that I was allowed to watch over him alone in this hour of crisis.

Mr. Churchill often made special mention of the effective care taken of him at this time by Lord Moran and Dr. Davis Evan Bedford, describing them as "This admirable M. and B."

THE voyage across to the Quebec Conference was made in the *Queen Mary*, and a very pleasant journey it was. One of the party was that remarkable man, Brigadier Orde Wingate, whose death a few weeks later was considered by Mr. Churchill to be a great loss to the Allies.

During the first weekend of the conference, we crossed into the United States to stay with the Roosevelts at Hyde Park.

At the station, as the train moved off, Mr. Churchill was about to light a cigar when a young coloured man ran towards us calling out, "Give me your cigar, sir, please give it to me!"

Winston took no notice for a time, but as the train gathered speed and the young man ran alongside, still pleading, he relented and tossed the cigar out of the window.

The negro caught it skilfully and danced with joy on the platform.

THE SECOND FRONT

ONE of the most pernicious agitations during the second half of the war was for the premature opening of a second front. It was promoted by the Communist party of Great Britain, whose members were given, or gave themselves, the task of trying to make all other war operations secondary to the relief of pressure on the Russian forces.

When Mr. Churchill saw walls and pavements chalked with demands to "Start the Second Front Now", he would growl, "Yes, we'll start – when we are ready."

Once I heard him say, "I do not intend to throw thousands of lives away unnecessarily. When the time is ripe, our preparations should ensure that our losses will not be too heavy."

The demand of the noisy minority had no effect at all on policy.

TROUBLE WITH A KETTLE

A HOUSEMAID once burnt out the element of an electric kettle, belonging to my wife, while we were at Chartwell. Mrs. Hill, the principal private secretary, put in a claim against the insurance company for the damage. In due course a cheque arrived in settlement.

When my wife took the cheque to Mr. Churchill to be endorsed, he looked at it carefully and then said, "I don't see that the insurance company is liable for this. Your kettle is not covered by my policy. That cheque must go back."

He then drew an equivalent cheque on his own, personal account and handed it to her. He was quite prepared to ensure that she should not be the loser, but he was equally determined that nothing was to be obtained from the insurance company to which he was not legally and morally entitled.

AT SOUTHAMPTON WATER

A s D DAY drew near, Mr. Churchill became even more energetic than was his habit. He was in and out of S.H.A.E.F. headquarters on the outskirts of London constantly, and he visited troops all over the country who were to participate in the invasion.

The day of 12th May 1944 was a notable one for the towns of Lydd, Camber, Rye, Bexhill and Hastings. They were visited by four Dominion Prime Ministers: Mr. Churchill, Mr. Mackenzie King of Canada, Field-Marshal Smuts of South Africa and Sir Godfrey Huggins of Southern Rhodesia.

At Hastings the Prime Minister and Mr. Mackenzie King were taken to some cliffs. Mr. Churchill, gazing across the Channel, said to the Mayor, "How far is it from here to the French coast?"

"About sixty miles," replied the Mayor.

"What are we waiting for? Let's get started and get at 'em!" countered Mr. Churchill.

At last he stood at Southampton, watching the troops embarking for the great but hazardous adventure. Many of them touched his coat as they passed and called for a speech. He did not want to speak, for he was too full of emotion, so he just called out, "Good luck, boys!"

A soldier questioned him, "Have you got your ticket, sir?"

"What ticket?" asked Mr. Churchill.

"One like this, sir," said the soldier, holding up a piece of paper. "It entitles me to a free trip to France."

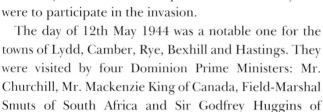

"I wish I had. If only I were a few years younger, nothing would keep me away."

Both the Prime Minister and his friend Mr. Ernest Bevin, who was with him, were visibly affected, and the tears ran down their faces.

Once only was he prevailed upon to make a speech, and that was a short one just before he returned to London. Mr. Churchill climbed slowly on to a paddle-wheel and with deep emotion started, "The time has come for you to liberate Europe. Good luck and God-speed to you."

He went on to speak of better conditions in Britain on their return, and as he finished, a Cockney voice from a troopship broke the tension with the cry, "And we don't want no dole, neither."

Churchill inspecting the *Queen Mary* in 1942.
Throughout the war Churchill's visits to the troops
had a miraculous effect on British morale.

The Prime Minister landed in France very soon after D Day. I was with him and he was overjoyed to witness the spectacular success of the invasion.

We returned on the destroyer *Kelvin*, and instead of setting course for home we sailed along the coast, about six miles out, until we were opposite the German artillery defences.

An order rang out and we fired several salvoes into the German positions. No reply came, and we turned for Portsmouth.

General Smuts later said to the Prime Minister, "I think the captain of the ship was rather cross with you for ordering him to fire on the German batteries."

"Why?" asked Mr. Churchill.

"Because, the destroyer was well within range of the German guns and they might have fired at us."

"That's what I did it for. I wanted them to fire."

A Tablecloth to the Rescue

AFTER his serious illness in Tunis, the Prime Minister went to convalesce at Marrakesh. It was a time of relaxation, and one glorious day a large party of us had a picnic lunch in the foothills.

A hundred feet below ran a mountain stream. Mr. Churchill said that he was going to climb down to it. Lord Moran objected, but Winston insisted that he felt strong enough and down he went quite safely.

On the way back I went first with Mr. Churchill. He held on to me and we made heavy going of it. Then I heard a shout.

Lady Diana Duff Cooper was hurrying down the cliff with a large tablecloth.

"Put this round him," she suggested.

We did. My colleague and I took an end each, and without causing any strain on Mr. Churchill, we had him to the top in no time.

This was certainly not the first time Tommy carried Churchill. He called Churchill "Father" but he was strong enough to carry him like a baby and would often put him to bed.

THE DEATH OF ROOSEVELT

As 1945 progressed the Prime Minister became more and more cheerful. Although he was feeling the strain, he could see daily the carefully laid plans of the Allies moving towards an inevitably successful conclusion. The war in Europe was drawing to a close and he knew that the means were available to deal Japan a knockout blow.

Then, on 12th April, came tragedy.

It was three o'clock in the morning when the Prime Minister's bell rang in my room. I went at once to his bedroom, and through the half-open door I heard his voice saying, "Terrible, terrible."

When I entered he was walking across the floor with his head bowed. When he turned to look at me, I saw that there were tears running down his cheeks.

"Have you heard the awful views, Thompson?" he said.

I replied, "No, sir."

"President Roosevelt has passed away," he told me.

After a little while he went on, "No one realises what he meant to this country and to the world. He was a great friend to us. He gave us immeasurable help at a time when we most needed it. I may, I hope, be able to go across to the funeral, which takes place this weekend. I do not know for certain yet."

On Friday evening, as he went to bed, he again spoke to me of Mr. Roosevelt. "I have lost a good friend and one who got things done. We now have to start all over again." His grief was moving.

The Prime Minister had seen so much of the American President during the war years, and their minds had

Churchill and Roosevelt in 1943.

always been in harmony. Mr. Roosevelt had seemed an ill man at Yalta, but had persevered bravely in the task of preparing the peace. No man had done more for victory, and he died just as the prize was in the grasp of the Allies.

For myself may I say that I shall always remember, even more than his statesmanship, his gracious, kindly way, his love of the humble and the weak, and, above all, the deep humility with which he strove to serve his fellow men.

THE END OF MUSSOLINI

THE last days of the war in Europe were great days to have lived through at the side of the British leader.

Every twenty-four hours seemed to bring fresh news of triumph. Mr. Churchill lived in a continual whirl of success. It was certain beyond a peradventure that the victory to which he and millions of others had devoted years of their lives was achieved.

One evening the Prime Minister arrived at Chequers, burst into the house and announced to his assembled guests, "Ah, the beast is dead."

That was how we heard of Mussolini's end.

A Tough Job on V.E. Day

Throughout 7th May 1945 Mr. Churchill waited impatiently, hoping that he would be able to announce officially the end of the war. He was disappointed. President Truman and Marshal Stalin were in constant telephone conversation with the British Prime Minister and the upshot was that the decision was taken to make the formal announcement at 3 p.m. on 8th May.

Mr. Churchill was not pleased at the delay, and as he began to sense the impatience of the vast crowds that were assembling in central London waiting for news, he became more and more appreciative of their legitimate curiosity. He could not announce that the war was over, so he did the next best thing – he announced that the following day would be V.E. Day.

It was a memorable day for me. I have never worked harder than I did on 8th May 1945, for it was a mighty task to preserve Winston from his friends.

At 3 p.m. he drove from Downing Street to the House of Commons. The car was literally forced through the crowds. No engine power was necessary. Everyone seemed determined to shake the Prime Minister by the hand. Mr. Churchill was in his element. I was not so happy!

After the Thanksgiving Service at St. Margaret's, we left Westminster for Buckingham Palace. On the way Winston asked me for a cigar, but in the excitement I had forgotten to bring his case. He laughed and said, "Drive to the Annexe and I will get one. I must put one on for them. They expect it."

Protecting Churchill from friend or foe on V.E. Day.

Later he appeared on the balcony at the Ministry of Health and addressed a seething, wildly enthusiastic mass of people. He had with him his grandson, Julian Sandys, and Mr. Churchill joined with the people in singing "Land of Hope and Glory" – indeed, he conducted them as they did so.

As he reached his peroration, he said dramatically, "The lights went out," whereupon, quite accidentally, the floodlights that were upon him from the opposite side of the road went dim. The crowd roared with laughter, and when he realised what had happened, he joined in before he brought his speech to a conclusion. That was the signal for a fresh outburst of sustained cheering.

V. E. Plus One

I HAD hoped that I might have the evening off the night after V.E. Day. The dense crowds in London had been an immense strain, and I felt sure that Mr. Churchill would feel in need of a rest. I was disappointed.

In the morning I had been called to make out a drive through the West End taking in the United States and Soviet Embassies. I did this and we motored through the streets of London for a couple of hours in an open car accompanied by an escort of mounted police.

When we got back to Downing Street at about 6 p.m., I assumed that Mr. Churchill was in for the night and dismissed the open car.

At 8.30 p.m. Winston decided to go out again. He looked down his nose at the saloon I called up, and queried, "Where is that open car?"

I replied with some trepidation, "It has gone, sir."

Angrily Mr. Churchill retorted, "All right then, I shall just walk."

"Impossible, sir," I objected. "The crowd is too dense."

I might as well not have spoken. Off he started and with him I had to go. Two saloons followed on my signal.

When we reached Whitehall, he realised that he could not get through and announced, "I shall walk between the two cars."

I begged him to wait for the mounted police as the crowd was closing in, but he refused. He was taking no notice of anything I said that evening. He was still peeved because I had sent the open car away.

Suddenly he decided to climb on the top of the car, which I felt he might have done earlier with advantage. He sat on the roof with his feet dangling over the windscreen. He looked very funny, and his irritation left him immediately.

Later he addressed another vast crowd from the balcony of the Downing Street Annexe. He spoke seriously for a time, and then with sudden inspiration he said, "I am going to recite a verse of 'Rule Britannia'. Then you must sing it." As he concluded his verse, he raised his arm and started the first note of the song.

The crowd took it up with gusto, and with the sound of the voices ringing in his ears, he went inside.

Tommy did finally manage to snatch some time to celebrate the end of the war with his children. By this time he was divorced from his wife Kate, and just four weeks after V.E. Day he married Mary Shearburn.

"If They Throw Me Out"

B Y APRIL 1945 the strain of organising victory and the continual round of conferences, together with his routine work in the House of Commons, were taking their toll of Mr. Churchill's strength. Those of us nearest to him were becoming increasingly alarmed at his health.

On 9th April, a beautiful, sunny day, he looked out of the windows at his beloved Chartwell and said to me, knowing that a General Election could not be long delayed, "Well, Thompson, if they throw me out in three months' time, I shall come down here again and be as happy as a sandboy."

Knowing Winston as I did, the thought flashed through my mind: I wonder how long you would be happy with no political work to do?

By the end of the war, Tommy had become personally famous among the police forces of the world. When Churchill was defeated in the General Election and no longer required Tommy's services, Tommy began touring the United States and Canada to talk about British policing methods. In between trips abroad he sat down to write his memoirs. It took him six years to get *I Was Churchill's Shadow* approved for publication by Scotland Yard and Churchill, and it was vetted and changed many times.

WINSTON CHURCHILL.

"England! Awake!" - a voice cried. But we slept
nAnd heedednot the voice of those who died.
That we might live.....the silent shadows crept
Nearer and ever nearer to our side.
The war-machines of others did not sleep -
Lulled by a sense of false security -
Their constant watch they dared not fail to keep
Until their plans should reach maturity.
But we - in splendid blindness - did not hear
The voice that would disturb our foolish peace.
The vision of one man - though crystal clear -
Urged us to waken - urged and would not cease....
Throughout the years of conflict he'd foretold
He led us - faithfully and certainly.
Through the long night - when even hope grew cold
He never failed us - surely, patiently,
He steered us through our country's darkest hour,
Till the far-distant, shining goal was won.
And Britain, in her reborn strength and power
Will not forget the courage of her son.
And we, whose lives and liberties we owe
Must yet remember all that might have been
And yet may be if we should fail again
To keep the course that he has made so plain.
All honour to the man whose steady hand
Guided us through the turmoil and the strife
And drove the hordes from our beloved land
Giving us freedom, hope reborn and life.
Aparing no effort in his ceaseless round
Giving his every moment, thought and deed.
May we remember in our peace new found
The man who never failed us in our need.

15. 5. 45

An unsigned poem found among Mary Shearburn
and Walter's papers.

Inspecting bomb damage at Birkenhead with Walter
Thompson beside him in the front seat of the car.

PICTURE SOURCES

Numbers refer to pages.

ACKNOWLEDGEMENTS

I would like to thank Bernard Dow for the great silhouettes and for
being a lovely Dad, Harold Thompson for his memories and
photographs, Jan Glass for her little suitcase full of memories,
Peggy Vance for her support and tenacity, Lesley James for being
a great networker and friend, Kit Whitfield for her close reading,
and Gordon Smith for being my rock.

LINDA STOKER

Sunday Dispatch, MAY 27, 1945

CHURCHILL'S
SHAD[O]

By WALTER H. THOMPSON

WALTER H. THOMP-
SON is not a name
you will see very
often. But you are seeing
pictures of Walter H.
Thompson nearly every
day; as often, in fact, as
you see pictures of Mr.
Winston Churchill.

For Detective-Inspector W. H.
Thompson is the Prime Minister's "shadow," the bodyguard who is going to be busier
in the next six months than he
has ever been in all the 30
years or so since he joined the
Special Branch of Scotland
Yard.

ston Churchill's private country
residence near Westerham, Kent.

Under the very personal direction of the man who was later to
build up the greatest defensive
and offensive structure Britain
has ever known, Walter Thompson helped four small children—
Diana, Randolph, Sarah, and Mary
Churchill—to construct what was
probably the biggest and most
elaborate sand-castle ever erected
on the shores of Britain.

That was incidental—but not
trivial—in the work of the man
who came out of retirement in
1940, at the special request of Mr.
Churchill, to act once more as personal bodyguard. For Walter
Thompson, who began his
"watchdog" career with Mr.
Lloyd George at the Spa Conference, had retired ten years previously.

He had, in fact, written
memoirs in 1938 and they in-
cluded intimate pen-pictures
only of Churchill and
George but of a hundred and
foreign potentates who
State visits to this country
handed over to him as his
particular "cares."

Thompson is [...]
to look at this [...]
with no very [...]
except a pair [...]
blue, keen e[...]
think so. Y[...]
his career [...]
Churchill [...]
sort to to [...]
puts tac[...]

As w[...]
it is [...]
else, [...]
auto[...]
trib[...]
of [...]

Going Places

WHEN, in newspapers,
or on the screen of
your local cinema,
you see pictures of
Mr. Churchill, you will find just
behind one of his shoulders a man
who has a detached, almost
apologetic air as if somehow he
had "gate-crashed" on the particular event and, having little
interest in its significance, was
just hanging around because he
'd not know what else to do
't it.
sombre, in negative-
and dark felt hat,
rolled umbrella
on, who in
will be
ton

Gangster

IT was i[...]
of Wa[...]
"a c[...]
care [...]
Yard [...]
igit[...]